Cordon Bleu

Dinner
Parties

Cordon Bleu

Dinner
Parties

 CBC / B.P.C. Publishing Ltd.

Published by
B.P.C. Publishing Ltd.,
P.O. Box 20,
Abingdon, Oxon.

Designed by Melvyn Kyte
Printed and bound in England
by Waterlow (Dunstable) Limited

These recipes have been adapted from the Cordon Bleu Cookery Course
published by Purnell in association with the London Cordon Bleu Cookery
School
Principal : Rosemary Hume ; Co-Principal : Muriel Downes

Contents

Introduction

Party time is here again and we give you another selection of planned menus for when you are entertaining. We have suggested menus for up to twelve people, which we hope for your sakes will be the most you will have to entertain to a full scale dinner party !

There are menus in this book for novice and advanced cooks, for occasions when you have all day to prepare a meal and for those when your time is strictly limited. Whichever you choose, they should all be fun to eat and fun to prepare. Timetables are provided to guide you through the order of preparation for each meal so that when your guests arrive you can be cool and sociable, confidant that all is well under way in the kitchen. And to give you some choice without sacrificing the benefits of the timetables, there are alternatives within most of the menus.

In our appendix, we have included a glossary of cooking terms used and notes and recipes for basic items mentioned in the special menus.

Experienced cooks may not need to use this, but if there is anything you do not understand in a recipe you will probably find it further explained in the appendix.

Cooking for large numbers can be extremely hard work, or it can be great fun if you are a true Cordon Bleu cook at heart. Pick your menu carefully to suit the occasion and your own energies, and plan ahead to make it a pleasure for yourself and your guests.

Rosemary Hume
Muriel Downes

You will find that cooking times given in individual recipes in this book have sometimes been adapted in the timetables to help you when cooking and serving a three-course meal.

Menu 1 Beef

Serves 4

Starter : Fish croquettes with Dutch sauce

Main course : Tournedos à la russe, Parisienne potatoes, Haricots verts

---

Dessert : Soufflé Monte Cristo

Alternative starter : Herrings in white wine

TIMETABLE

Day before
Make chocolate caraque and macaroons.
Turn olives for tournedos.

Morning
Make soufflé and put aside to set.
Cut tournedos and marinate.
Prepare fish croquettes ready for frying and leave on a large plate with a thin layer of extra crumbs underneath them.
(Or marinate herrings and prepare dressing).
Prepare potato balls for parisienne potatoes and leave, covered with cold water.

Assemble ingredients and equipment for final cooking from 6.00 for dinner around 8 pm.

Order of work

6.00 Fry croquettes and parsley and set aside. Prepare mushrooms for cooking.

6.30 Make mushroom salpicon, omitting soured cream, and fry croûtes.

7.00 Make Dutch sauce ; after simmering for 1-2 minutes tip into a double saucepan (or basin standing in a pan of hot water) to keep warm — do not add yolks and lemon at this stage.

7.15 Set oven at 300°F or Mark 2. Cook potatoes.

7.30 Put croquettes and parsley on crumpled absorbent kitchen paper on a baking tin in oven to heat. Complete salpicon and dish up tournedos, keep warm.
(Dish up herrings, adding dressing, apples and rice.)

8.00 Beat egg yolks into Dutch sauce, add lemon and reheat. Serve first course.

Fish croquettes

1 lb fresh haddock fillet
salt and pepper
juice of $\frac{1}{4}$ lemon
$\frac{1}{2}$ pint milk (infused with 1
    slice of onion, 1 blade of mace,
    $\frac{1}{2}$ bayleaf, 6 peppercorns)
1$\frac{1}{2}$ oz butter
1$\frac{1}{2}$ oz plain flour
1 rounded teaspoon gelatine
    (soaked in 1 tablespoon
    cold water)
1 egg (beaten)

For frying
2-3 tablespoons seasoned flour
1 egg (beaten)
dried white breadcrumbs
bunch of parsley (well washed
    and dried) — to garnish

*Deep fat bath or pan, and basket;
square cake tin, or oval pie dish*

Method

Set oven at 325°F or Mark 3. Wash and dry the fish, place in a buttered, ovenproof dish, season and add a squeeze of lemon juice. Cover with buttered paper and cook for 10-12 minutes in the pre-set oven.

Infuse the milk with the flavourings in a pan, then strain and set aside to cool. Meanwhile flake the fish, removing the skin and bones.

Melt the butter in a small saucepan, stir in the flour off the heat and blend in the strained milk, beating well to avoid lumps. Season and stir over gentle heat until boiling ; then simmer for 1 minute. Add the flaked fish a little at a time, beating the mixture well. This breaks the fibres of the fish and helps the mixture to bind. Add the soaked gelatine to the hot fish mixture, stir until dissolved and well distributed. (The small

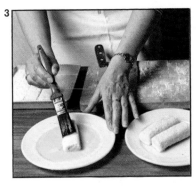

1 *When chilled and firm, cut fish mixture into 3-inch long strips*
2 *Roll the strips into small cork-shaped croquettes on a floured board, using two palette knives*
3 *Brush the croquettes with a little beaten egg before rolling them in the dried breadcrumbs*

quantity of gelatine is not detectable when the croquettes are served hot, but makes the mixture much easier to handle when cold.)

Add the beaten egg and taste for seasoning. Turn mixture into a square cake tin or oval pie dish and leave to cool. Then place in refrigerator until really chilled and firm.

Cut chilled mixture into strips about 3 inches long and 1 inch wide and deep. Roll them with two palette knives into neat cork-shaped croquettes on a floured board. Use as little seasoned flour as possible and avoid working it into the fish mixture. Brush each croquette with beaten egg and roll in the breadcrumbs. Heat the fat or oil to 375°F.

Watchpoint Before you start frying, make absolutely sure that you have enough fat in the pan to cover the croquettes. Unless they are covered with the hot fat to seal the coating, the croquettes will burst when first put in oven for reheating.

Fry the croquettes until golden-brown, drain well, then turn carefully on to absorbent paper. Turn the heat off and leave the fat 2-3 minutes to cool a little. Put the parsley in the fat basket and lower it very gently into the fat; don't immerse it until the violent spluttering stops. When the bubbling stops, drain the parsley well; it should still be bright green and very crisp.

Serve the Dutch sauce separately.

When frying the croquettes make sure that the fat covers them completely to seal the coating

Dutch sauce

¾ pint milk (infused with 1 slice
    of onion, ½ bayleaf, 6 peppercorns)
1½ oz butter
1¼ oz plain flour
salt
2 egg yolks
juice of ½ lemon

Method
Infuse the milk with the flavourings, then strain into a bowl.

Melt the butter in a small saucepan, remove from the heat and blend in the flour and strained milk. Add salt to taste and stir mixture over gentle heat until boiling. Simmer for 1-2 minutes.

Draw pan away from the heat, allow to cool very slightly then beat in the egg yolks. Reheat without boiling and add the lemon juice. Taste for seasoning. Use immediately.

Tournedos à la russe

6 tournedos, or 1½-2 lb beef fillet
1-2 tablespoons brandy, or dry
  sherry
black pepper (ground from mill)
clarified butter (for frying)
6 croûtes of bread (cut to fit the
  tournedos)

For salpicon
10 oz even-size flat mushrooms
about 1½ oz butter
salt and pepper
¾ wineglass of red, or white, wine,
  or jellied stock
6-8 green olives (turned)
juice of ½ lemon
3-4 tablespoons soured cream

Method
If using fillet of beef, trim the fillet and cut 6 tournedos from the centre. Lay these, or the tournedos prepared by the butcher, on a dish, sprinkle with the brandy (or sherry) and grind over the black pepper. Set aside for about 1 hour.

When ready to cook, peel the mushrooms and cut the stalks level with the caps. Sauté them quickly in the butter, season, add the wine (or stock) and allow it to reduce a little.

Tournedos à la russe, with its olive and mushroom salpicon, is dished up with haricots verts and parisienne potatoes

Draw pan aside.

Heat the clarified butter in a large frying pan, fry the croûtes in this and then dish them up. Pour off and reserve any butter. Reheat the pan, add a little more clarified butter, together with the reserved butter, put in the tournedos and fry rapidly for 3-3$\frac{1}{2}$ minutes on each side.

While the tournedos are cooking, add the olives, lemon juice and soured cream to the mushrooms and shake the pan to mix them (stirring might break the olives and mushrooms). Reheat this salpicon, adding any marinade left from the tournedos. Dish up the tournedos on the croûtes and surround with the salpicon of mushrooms and olives. Serve very hot with parisienne potatoes and haricots verts.

Parisienne potatoes

Scoop out potato balls with a cutter, plain boil them, toss in melted butter, or sauté them ; add chopped parsley.

Tournedos are cut from the eye of the fillet of beef and should be not less than 1-1$\frac{1}{2}$ inches thick ; though expensive, they have little or no waste. They are best cooked rare to medium to allow for the dish to be kept hot. They may be dry-fried or grilled before serving with an appropriate garnish, and dished up on a croûte of fried bread, cut to fit exactly, or on a circle of duchesse potatoes or chestnut purée. The idea is not only to raise the tournedos on the dish (for better presentation), but also to absorb any juices from the meat.

To turn olives

This is done to remove the stones from green olives without spoiling their shape. Make a small cut across the top of the olive (but not right through) with a small sharp knife. Then, keeping the blade of the knife against the stone, work in a spiral removing the flesh as you go until you get to the base of the stone, then remove the flesh from the bottom. Reshape the olive. (Black olives, being soft, can be stoned by slitting down one side and using the point of a small knife to lever out the stone.)

Soufflé Monte Cristo

3 eggs (separated)
2½ oz caster sugar
½ vanilla pod (split)
¾ pint milk
2-3 drops of vanilla essence
    (optional)
½ oz gelatine
2½ fl oz water
7½ fl oz double cream (lightly
    whisked)
chocolate caraque (made from
    2 oz plain chocolate)
5 almond macaroons
little brandy, or rum, or liqueur
    (such as Cointreau, or Grand
    Marnier)
¼ pint double cream (more if liked)
    — for decoration

*6-inch diameter top (No. 2 size)
soufflé dish ; ½ lb jam jar*

Method

Tie a band of greaseproof paper around the dish so that it extends above the rim by about 3 inches, and grease the inside of the paper. Lightly oil the jam jar and put it in the centre of the soufflé dish.

Put the egg yolks into a basin, place over a pan of hot water and beat with the sugar until light and fluffy, while infusing vanilla pod in the milk in a pan. When milk is at scalding point, remove pod and pour the milk on to the yolk mixture. Return to the pan and stir over gentle heat until the custard thickens creamily and will coat the back of the spoon. Strain and cool. If necessary, add 2-3 drops of vanilla essence to strengthen the flavour.

Soak and dissolve the gelatine in the water and add to the

The thickened soufflé mixture and chocolate caraque are layered into the prepared soufflé dish with the jam jar in the centre

Chocolate caraque

Grate 3 oz plain block chocolate or chocolate couverture (cooking chocolate). Melt on a plate over hot water and work with a palette knife until smooth. Spread this thinly on a marble slab or laminated surface and leave until nearly set. Then, using a long sharp knife, shave it off the slab, slantwise, using a slight sawing movement and holding the knife almost upright. The chocolate will form long scrolls or flakes. These will keep in an airtight tin but look better when they are freshly made.

custard. Turn the mixture into a thin pan and stand this on ice, or in iced water, and stir with a metal spoon until the mixture is thickening. Then remove from the ice and fold in the lightly whipped cream and, finally, the stiffly whisked egg whites. Pour the soufflé mixture quickly into the soufflé dish, layering it with chocolate caraque, keeping some in reserve for decoration. Leave in a cool place, or in the refrigerator, to set.

Watchpoint A lump or two of ice put into the jam jar will help the soufflé to set more quickly if you are pressed for time.

Meanwhile break up the macaroons and sprinkle them well with the chosen spirit or liqueur. When ready to serve, gently twist the jam jar and lift it out carefully. Immediately fill the cavity with the macaroons. Pipe the extra whipped cream round the edge and decorate with remaining chocolate caraque.

Soufflé Monte Cristo is decorated with whipped cream and chocolate caraque. The centre hole (made with a jam jar) is filled with macaroons

Herrings in white wine

2 herring fillets in wine (these
  can be bought in most
  delicatessens)
lemon juice, or wine vinegar
salt and pepper
2 tablespoons long grain rice
2-3 tablespoons oil
1 tablespoon wine vinegar
1 teaspoon made English mustard
2 medium-size dessert apples
  (Cox or Pippin)
lettuce leaves

Method
Cut the herring fillets in diagonal strips, sprinkle them well with lemon juice (or vinegar) and season. Leave for at least 1 hour. Boil the rice in plenty of salted water, drain and dry.

When ready to serve, mix the oil and vinegar together, season well, add the mustard and mix this dressing with the herrings. Peel and slice apples and add to the herrings with the rice. Serve in a bowl or on lettuce leaves on individual plates.

Menu 2 Beef

Starter : Smoked salmon rolls with prawns

Main course : Fillet of beef italienne, Gnocchi romana

Dessert : Rich fig pudding with hard sauce

Alternative main course : Pheasant smetana, Boiled rice

TIMETABLE

Day before
Buy prawns and keep in
refrigerator to thaw out.
Make the mayonnaise.
Make gnocchi romana but do
not cut. Make the hard sauce
and demi-glace sauce.

Afternoon
Assemble equipment and
ingredients for final cooking
from 3.00 for dinner around
8 pm.

Order of work

3.00 Make pudding and put on
to steam (if pressure
cooking, make at 5.00).
(Boil rice, drain, dry and
put in dish ready for
reheating.)

5.30 Prepare salmon rolls, cut
brown bread and butter.
Dish up and cover with
dampened greaseproof
paper.
Cut gnocchi and arrange
in dish with butter and
cheese, ready for
browning.

6.15 (Start pheasants. Complete
by 7.15 and leave ready
for reheating.)

7.00 Start beef, complete by
7.45 and leave in covered
pan until ready to serve.

7.30 Set oven at 400°F or
Mark 6.
Cook French beans (put
on rice to reheat).

7.45 Brown gnocchi in pre-set
oven.
(Reheat pheasants and
dish up.) Dish up the beef
and the pudding.

8.00 Serve first course.

Smoked salmon rolls with prawns

Starter

8 oz smoked salmon (8-10 good
slices)
10 oz shelled prawns (frozen)
good $\frac{1}{4}$ pint thick mayonnaise
3-4 drops of Tabasco sauce
$\frac{1}{2}$ teaspoon paprika pepper
$\frac{1}{2}$ teaspoon tomato purée
1 dessertspoon double cream
(optional)
To serve
8 wedges of lemon
brown bread and butter

Method
Leave salmon in the paper in
which it was bought, and roughly
chop prawns. Blend mayonnaise
with Tabasco sauce, paprika
pepper, tomato purée and cream,
if used. Bind the prawns together with the mayonnaise and
divide the mixture among the
slices of salmon. Place one
portion on each salmon slice
and roll up. Dish up on individual plates, with a wedge of
lemon on each.

Serve with brown bread and
butter, and provide a small fork
for easy eating.

*Left : rolling up a slice of smoked
salmon with prawn and mayonnaise
filling*
*Below : smoked salmon rolls, with
lemon and brown bread and butter*

Fillet of beef italienne

Main course

3 lb fillet of beef
3 oz button mushrooms (sliced)
½ oz butter
good dripping, or butter
1 onion (quartered)
1 carrot (quartered)
bouquet garni
1 dessertspoon chopped parsley
2 oz lean cooked ham (sliced and
   shredded)

For sauce
1 shallot (finely chopped)
¼ pint white wine
½ pint demi-glace sauce
1 dessertspoon tomato purée

1 *Adding the sauce to browned fillet of beef before cooking on top of stove*
2 *Adding cooked mushrooms, parsley and ham to the medium-rare fillet of beef*

Method

Sauté the mushrooms in ½ oz butter, then take out and put in the shallot and wine. Reduce to half, then add the demi-glace sauce and tomato purée. Bring to the boil and simmer for 3-4 minutes to a syrupy consistency. Cover and draw aside.

Brown the beef quickly all over in dripping or butter, with the onion and carrot in a large pan. Then pour off any fat, add the bouquet garni and sauce. Cover tightly and simmer gently on top of stove for about 20-25 minutes (7 minutes to the lb), turning once or twice. The meat should be medium-rare.

Draw pan aside, remove bouquet garni, add the cooked mushrooms, parsley and ham. Keep pan covered until ready to serve. Serve with French beans and a dish of well-browned gnocchi romana.

Fillet of beef italienne continued

Gnocchi romana

1 medium-size onion (peeled)
1 bayleaf
$\frac{1}{2}$ pint milk
$\frac{1}{2}$ pint water
5 rounded tablespoons maize meal,
  or coarse semolina
salt and pepper
$\frac{1}{2}$ teaspoon French mustard
1 oz butter
2 oz cheese (grated)

Method

Put onion, bayleaf, milk and water into a pan, cover and bring very slowly to the boil. Take out onion and bayleaf.

Draw pan aside and stir in the maize meal (or semolina). Return pan to heat and stir until boiling ; season, and, if too thick, add more liquid. The consistency should be that of thick porridge. **Watchpoint** The amount of milk and water varies according to the type and coarseness of the maize meal used.

Continue to simmer, stirring frequently, for 7-10 minutes. Draw pan aside, adjust seasoning, then add mustard, butter and three-quarters of the grated cheese. Turn out on a tray or flat dish so that the mixture spreads to a thickness of $\frac{1}{2}$-$\frac{3}{4}$ inch (the mixture should just pour, the consistency of very thick cream). Leave for 2-3 hours or overnight if preferred. Turn the sheet of gnocchi on to a board or table and cut it into small squares, rounds or crescents. Arrange these in a well-buttered ovenproof dish in a circle, with the pieces overlapping. Sprinkle gnocchi generously with melted butter and scatter on the remaining cheese. Brown in oven,

pre-set at 400°F or Mark 6, for 10-15 minutes.

Fillet of beef italienne is garnished with mushrooms, parsley and ham, and served with a dish of well-browned gnocchi romana and French beans

Rich fig pudding with hard sauce

8 oz dried figs
4 oz raisins (stoned)
8 oz dates (stoned)
3 oz stem ginger
2-3 tablespoons brandy, or rum
6 oz fresh white breadcrumbs
8 oz self-raising flour
6 oz shredded suet
good pinch of salt
3 eggs
grated rind and juice of 1 lemon
a little milk (optional)
maple syrup (optional)

Pudding basin (2 pints capacity)

Method
Slice the fruit and ginger, mix together and sprinkle with the brandy or rum. Cover and leave for 1 hour or longer. Mix well together the crumbs, flour, suet and salt. Beat the eggs to a froth and mix into the dry ingredients with the lemon rind and juice, and the fruit. Mix thoroughly, adding a little milk if necessary to bring the mixture to a dropping consistency.

Turn into well-greased basin and steam for 4 hours, or use a pressure cooker. Turn out, pour round a little maple syrup or serve with a hard sauce.

Hard sauce

For a brandy butter, take 4 oz unsalted butter, 4 oz caster sugar and 2-3 tablespoons brandy.

For rum butter, take 3 oz unsalted butter, 3 oz soft brown sugar, grated rind of $\frac{1}{2}$ lemon and squeeze of juice, and 2-3 tablespoons rum.

Cream butter thoroughly, gradually beat in sugar (and add lemon rind and juice for rum butter); continue beating until white, then add brandy (or rum), a teaspoon at a time, to flavour butter well. Work in a little chopped glacé ginger if liked. Pile up in a small dish and chill well before serving.

1 *Slicing the fruit and ginger before sprinkling with brandy*
2 *Adding the rum-flavoured fruit to the mixed breadcrumbs, flour, suet and salt*

Dessert

Figs and ginger make an unusual combination in this rich pudding

Pheasant smetana

2 pheasants (a brace, or 2 hen
  birds)
good 1 oz butter
2 shallots (chopped)
1 wineglass white wine
salt and pepper

For sauce
3 shallots (finely chopped)
1 large wineglass dry white wine
1 dessertspoon plain flour
$7\frac{1}{2}$ fl oz lightly soured cream (fresh
  cream with a little lemon juice
  added may be substituted)

Method

Heat the butter in a large pan,
and slowly brown the birds all
over. Then add shallots and
wine, season, cover and simmer
gently on top of the stove for
35-40 minutes, turning the birds
over from time to time.

When birds are cooked, pour
off the gravy from the pan and
reserve it, leaving birds in pan,
covered. To prepare the sauce,
cook shallots in the wine in a
saucepan until the wine has
reduced by half, then pour off
and set aside. Skim the butter
from the reserved gravy, put it
into the saucepan and stir in the
flour. Strain in the gravy, add
the reduced wine and the cream.
Season well and boil until sauce
is thick and creamy. Draw pan
aside.

Take up pheasants, carve into
joints and dish up. Reheat sauce
and strain over the dish. Serve
very hot with boiled rice and
French beans.

Menu 3 Beef

Starter : Mushroom soup

Main course : Steaks morateur, Chip potatoes

Dessert : Soufflé chinois

TIMETABLE

Order of work

Morning
Make soufflé (but do not decorate) and put in refrigerator.
Make soup and tip into a bowl to cool.
Cut potatoes and leave soaking in a bowl of water.
Put anchovies to soak in milk.

Assemble ingredients and equipment for final cooking from 6.00 for dinner around 8 pm.

6.00 Drain potatoes, wrap in a cloth and dry.
Take soufflé out of refrigerator, decorate and set aside.
Put soup into saucepan ready for reheating.
Set oven at 350°F or Mark 4 and put plates and dishes to heat in warming drawer.

7.15 Heat fat for potatoes. Give them their first fry, then drain.

7.30 Cook beans.
Reheat deep fat bath.
Give potatoes a second fry, leave on absorbent paper on a plate in the bottom of the oven to keep hot, and sprinkle with salt.

7.40 Make anchovy butter, cook steaks and make sauce.
Dish up steaks and chips, keep warm in oven.
Reheat soup.

8.00 Serve first course.

Mushroom soup

½ lb flat mushrooms
2 medium-size onions (chopped)
1½ oz butter
2 tablespoons plain flour
2 pints chicken stock
salt and pepper
1 tablespoon long grain rice
1 bayleaf
2 tablespoons watercress
    chopped)

Method

Wash the mushrooms quickly in a bowl of salted water, drain, and cut the stalks level with the mushrooms. Remove the peel. Chop the stalks and peelings finely and slice the mushrooms thinly.

Melt 1 oz of the butter in a pan, add the mushrooms and onions and sweat them (cover with buttered greaseproof paper, pressed well down, and the lid of the pan) ; cook them slowly for 5 minutes. Draw pan aside, remove lid and paper, add remaining butter and, when melted, blend in flour and stock.

Season, stir until boiling, add the rice and bayleaf. Cover and simmer for 15-20 minutes.

Remove the bayleaf, taste for seasoning, then add the watercress before serving.

Flat mushrooms (champignons) and button ones (champignons de Paris) are well known in Britain, but there are many other members of this family common to French cooking.

In the beautiful mountain region of Franche-Comté, better known as the Jura, the forests abound with wild mushrooms. Edible ones bear such exotic names as chanterelles, oronges, russules, cèpes and morilles.

Cèpes are extra fleshy mushrooms considered to be characteristic of the Languedoc. Morilles or morels are the most sought-after because of their delicate flavour. The best ones are dark brown, have a pointed top and a rather coarse surface like a sponge.

Make this soup with flat, dark mushrooms for a good flavour and colour

Steaks morateur

4 fillet steaks (each 1-inch thick)
$\frac{1}{2}$ oz butter (for frying)
1 shallot (finely chopped)
1 wineglass dry white wine
anchovy butter

Method
Set frying pan on full heat for 2-3 minutes before the butter is added and the cooking begins. (A very heavy cast-iron frying pan gives the best results ; if you don't possess this type of pan and are using an aluminium one, put 1 teaspoon of salad oil in it before heating for 2-3 minutes.)

Drop in the butter and as it foams put in the steaks. Press them down well with a palette knife and lower the heat slightly under the pan. Cook meat until well browned (about 3 minutes), then turn the steaks and cook on the other side for a further 3 minutes.

Place the steaks on a warm serving dish. Add the shallot to the pan, lower the heat and cook for 2-3 minutes. Pour on the wine and cook until it is reduced to half the quantity. Stir in the anchovy butter and simmer for an extra 2-3 minutes. Pour the sauce over the steaks and serve at once.

1 When frying the fillet steaks, put pan on full heat before adding butter ; as soon as this is foaming well, add steaks. Cook until they are well browned on both sides. Take out, keep warm on a hot serving dish
2 Make sauce by adding chopped shallot to the pan, then the wine, which is cooked until reduced to about half the quantity. Stir in the anchovy butter and simmer before pouring the sauce over steaks

Serve chip potatoes and French beans with these delicious steaks

Chip potatoes

2 lb even-size potatoes (weight
  after peeling)
deep fat, or oil (for frying)
salt

Deep fat bath, or pan, and basket

Method
Square off the ends and sides
of the potatoes, then cut down
into $\frac{1}{2}$-inch thick slices, then into
thick fingers. Soak in cold water
for about 30 minutes, then drain.
Wrap potatoes in absorbent
paper or a cloth and leave for
20-30 minutes.

Heat the fat, which should
not come more than two-thirds
of the way up the sides of the
pan. Dip in the frying basket
(this prevents food sticking).
Put potatoes in the basket (out
of the fat) ; when the fat reaches
the right temperature (350°F),
gently lower basket into it. If
you don't have a frying thermometer, drop in a finger of
potato ; if this rises to the surface of the fat straight away and
starts to bubble gently, the fat
is ready.

Fry gently until the potatoes
are just soft (pierce one with
the point of a knife to test) but
not coloured. Lift out and drain.
They can be left like this for a
short time before the final frying,
or while the steaks are cooking.

Reheat the fat to 400°F or
oil to 360-375°F. Carefully
lower in the basket of potatoes
and fry to a deep golden-brown.
Drain chips well on absorbent
paper, turn into a hot dish for
serving and sprinkle with salt.

The fat should be strained
through dry muslin when cool,

On the first frying, chips are cooked until they are just soft, then they are drained and set aside

After second frying in hotter fat, drain chips when golden, put in a hot dish and sprinkle with salt

Soufflé chinois

¾ pint milk
3 egg yolks
2 oz caster sugar
2 tablespoons syrup (from the
preserved ginger)
½ oz gelatine (soaked in 4 tablespoons cold water)
¼ pint double cream
3 egg whites
2 tablespoons preserved ginger
(sliced)

For decoration
few extra preserved ginger slices
pistachio nuts (finely chopped),
or almonds (browned) — optional

*6-inch diameter top (No. 2 size)
soufflé dish*

Method
Prepare soufflé dish by tying a
double-thickness band of greaseproof paper round the outside to
stand 3 inches above top and
grease.

Scald the milk in a pan.
Beat the egg yolks and sugar
together over gentle heat until
thick and light in colour, add
the ginger syrup and pour on
the hot milk. Return to the pan
and stir over a gentle heat until
the mixture thickens. Strain it
Into a bowl, add the soaked
gelatine and stir until it is
dissolved. Cover the bowl of
custard to prevent a skin forming
and allow to cool.

Whip the cream lightly until it
begins to thicken and whisk the
egg whites until stiff but not dry.
Turn the custard into a large
thin pan, stand this in a bowl of
cold water containing 3-4 ice
cubes and stir until the mixture
begins to thicken (a metal
saucepan cools it more quickly
than a china bowl).

Then take a metal spoon and

quickly fold in half the cream,
the sliced ginger and the
whisked egg whites. Stir very
carefully, holding the pan in the
ice-cold water, and as the mixture begins to thicken, turn it
into the prepared soufflé dish
and put in a cool place to set.

When set, peel away the
paper around soufflé dish. The
easiest and quickest way to do
this is to dip a palette or table
knife in very hot water and slip
it between the two thicknesses
of paper (the heat loosens them).

Whisk the remaining cream
and use to coat and decorate
the top of the soufflé. Sprinkle
with nuts, if wanted, and arrange
the extra ginger slices around
the top. (See photograph of
finished soufflé overleaf).

Watchpoint A cold soufflé with a
custard base made like this
should always be made the day
it is to be eaten.

*The custard is turned into a large,
thin pan resting on a bed of ice, to
cool it more quickly. Half the cream,
ginger and whisked egg whites are
folded in. When the mixture begins
to thicken, it is turned into the
soufflé dish*

Menu 4 Pork

Serves 4

Starter : Haddock Bercy

Main course : Roast pork dijonnaise, Cabbage alsacienne,
　　　　　　　Casserole of potatoes and onions

Dessert : Tarte aux pommes à l'orange

Alternative dessert : Crème blanche with cranberry compote

TIMETABLE

Order of work

Day before
Make flan pastry and store in
greaseproof paper in
refrigerator.
Cook and pulp apples but do
not add sugar and peel.
Make the apricot jam glaze.
(Make crème blanche and
cranberry compote.)

Morning
Line pastry into flan ring and
bake blind. Add sugar and
rind to apples and cook.
Slice oranges.
Shred cabbage and celery.
Prepare onions and potatoes
for casserole.
Make sauce for pork, strain
and leave in basin in a cool
place. Wash and trim
mushrooms but do not cook.
Prepare pork for baking.
Prepare fish and put in dish
ready for cooking. Prepare
tomatoes.
Cut bread croûtes, make
garlic butter and spread
over croûtes.
Finish flan.

Assemble ingredients for
·final cooking from 6.00 for
dinner around 8 pm.

6.00 Set oven for pork ;
assemble serving dishes
and plates.

6.15 Put pork in oven. Blanch
cabbage, add celery and
liquid and cook gently.
Start onions cooking for
casserole. Boil prepared
potatoes.

6.45 Baste and turn pork.
Chop shallot, boil in wine
to reduce quantity of liquid.
Sprinkle cooked cabbage
with parsley. Keep warm.
Sauté mushrooms for pork;
add to sauce, heat and
keep warm.

7.10 Put fish to cook on low
shelf in oven.
Baste pork.
Strain fish and keep warm.
Thicken sauce for fish.·
Heat canned potatoes and
add to casserole with
parsley. Put pork on
serving dish, turn oven to
low setting.

7.50 Toast croûtes, add cream,
parsley and tomatoes to
fish sauce and serve.

33

Haddock Bercy

1-1½ lb fresh haddock fillets
salt
squeeze of lemon juice
¼ pint water
6 peppercorns
2 tomatoes
1 shallot (finely chopped)
1 wineglass dry white wine
kneaded butter (made with 1 oz
   butter worked to a paste with
   ½ oz flour)
1 dessertspoon chopped parsley
1 tablespoon double cream

Method

Wash and dry fillets and place in a buttered ovenproof dish; sprinkle with salt, add the lemon and water and put in the peppercorns at one side. Cover with a buttered paper and poach in the oven, pre-set at 350°F or Mark 4, for about 15 minutes or until tender.

Scald and skin the tomatoes, cut in four, remove the seeds and cut flesh into neat shreds; keep on one side. Put the shallot in a pan with the wine, bring to the boil and reduce to half quantity. Strain on the liquid from the fish and thicken with the kneaded butter. Simmer for 2-3 minutes, adjust seasoning, add the parsley, cream and tomatoes and reheat gently.

Place the fish on a hot serving dish and spoon over the sauce. The dish may be garnished with crescent-shaped croûtes spread with garlic butter and toasted.

Haddock fillets with sauce spooned over and garnish of crescent-shaped croûtes spread with garlic butter before toasting.

Roast pork dijonnaise   Main course

3 lb loin of pork (chined)
3 tablespoons bacon fat
1 tablespoon dry mustard
   (English)
1 teaspoon caster sugar
1-2 dessertspoons white wine
3-4 tablespoons dried white
   breadcrumbs
12 cloves

For sauce
1 small onion (finely chopped)
$1\frac{1}{4}$ oz butter
1 tablespoon plain flour
$\frac{1}{2}$ pint well-flavoured stock
1 wineglass white wine
1 dessertspoon tomato purée
6 oz small flat mushrooms

The loin of pork is covered with bacon fat before spreading with a paste made from dry mustard, sugar and white wine

Method
Set oven at 375°F or Mark 6 (settings are not equal).

Trim off the excess fat from the pork, leaving just a $\frac{1}{4}$-$\frac{1}{2}$ inch wide rim and spread meat with 1 tablespoon of the bacon fat. Mix the mustard, sugar and wine to a paste, spread over the pork, then press on the crumbs and stud with the cloves.

Heat the remaining bacon fat in a roasting tin, put in the meat, baste well and cook for 25 minutes per lb and 25 minutes over.

Turn the meat after the first 30 minutes and baste about every 20 minutes.

To prepare sauce ; cook chopped onion in $\frac{3}{4}$ oz butter until soft, stir in the flour and brown well. Pour on the stock, add the wine and tomato purée and bring to the boil. Simmer sauce for 12-15 minutes, strain and return it to the rinsed pan.

Sauté the mushrooms in remaining butter for 1 minute only and add to the sauce. Put the pork on a serving dish and serve the sauce separately.

Roast pork dijonnaise continued

To accompany roast pork dijonnaise we suggest cabbage alsacienne and a casserole of onions and potatoes

Cabbage alsacienne

1 white Dutch cabbage (shredded)
1 oz butter
1 small head of celery (shredded)
1 wineglass dry white wine, or
　　same quantity of stock with
　　1 teaspoon wine vinegar
salt and pepper
1 tablespoon chopped parsley

Method
Blanch cabbage in pan of boiling salted water for 1 minute, then drain well.

Melt butter in a shallow pan or casserole, add celery and cook for 2-3 minutes. Add the cabbage and wine, or stock and wine vinegar. Season well, cover and cook gently for 25-30 minutes. Sprinkle with chopped parsley before serving.

Casserole of onions and potatoes

$\frac{3}{4}$ lb button onions
1 oz butter
1 teaspoon granulated sugar
$\frac{1}{2}$ pint stock
1 lb new potatoes (scraped),
　　or 1 lb old potatoes (peeled and
　　cut into small pieces), or 1 can
　　new potatoes
1 teaspoon chopped parsley
　　(optional)

Method
Blanch onions by putting in pan of cold water and bringing to boil ; strain before further cooking. Return to a flameproof casserole with butter, sugar and stock. Boil gently until onions are tender and stock has reduced to about 2 tablespoons. Do not allow onions to brown.

Cook potatoes in boiling salted water, or heat canned ones. Drain and add to the onions with parsley. Serve in the casserole.

37

Tarte aux pommes à l'orange

For French flan pastry
4 oz plain flour
2 oz caster sugar
2 egg yolks
2 oz butter
2-3 drops of vanilla essence

For filling
2 lb cooking apples (quartered,
cored and sliced)
3-4 tablespoons granulated sugar
grated rind of 2 oranges

To finish
2 seedless oranges (sliced in
rounds)
3-4 tablespoons apricot glaze

7-8 inch diameter flan ring

Method
First prepare pastry : sift flour
on to a slab or board. Make a
well in the centre and put in the
rest of the ingredients ; work to
a paste with the fingertips, then
draw in the flour quickly and
knead until smooth. Chill pastry
in refrigerator for at least 30
minutes.

Set oven at 375°F or Mark 5.
Roll out pastry and line flan ring.
Put in some uncooked rice (or
beans) on greaseproof paper
(to prevent pastry sides falling
in) and bake blind in pre-set
oven for 15 minutes.

Meanwhile prepare filling :
slice apples into a buttered pan,
cover with a tight fitting lid and
cook to a pulp. Rub through a
strainer and return purée to the
pan with sugar and orange rind.
Cook until thick, stirring all the
time. Turn out and cool a little.

Fill the flan case with the
apple purée and smooth over
the top. Cut peel and pith from
the oranges, slice into rounds
and arrange on top of the flan.

1 *To make French flan pastry , make
a well in sieved flour, put in sugar,
egg yolks, butter and vanilla essence*
2 *Then, using the fingertips of one
hand only, work all these added
ingredients to a smooth paste*
3 *Draw in the flour quickly, kneading
the mixture lightly until smooth ;
chill pastry before using*

38

Brush the oranges with warm glaze. Leave to set ; serve cold.

Apricot glaze gives an attractive golden finish to this flan

Crème blanche

Alternative dessert

1 **pint milk**
2 **tablespoons granulated sugar**
1 **vanilla pod**
5 **egg whites**
$\frac{1}{2}$ **pint double cream**

For cranberry compote
1 **lb cranberries**
8 **oz granulated sugar**
$\frac{1}{2}$ **pint water**
1 **lb dessert apples**

6-inch diameter (No. 2 size) oven-proof china, or glass, soufflé dish

Method

Set the oven at 375°F or Mark 5. Put the milk, sugar and vanilla pod in a pan and heat gently until the sugar is dissolved ; cover and leave to infuse for 5 minutes. Lightly whisk the egg whites with a fork, just enough to make them smooth but not fluffy : strain on the milk and leave to cool. Then add half the cream. Pour mixture into the soufflé dish, cover with grease-proof paper or foil and cook in a bain-marie in the pre-set oven, for about 35-40 minutes until set. Leave until cold. Turn out, mask with remaining cream, lightly whipped.

Dissolve sugar in the water over gentle heat, then boil for 2-3 minutes to make a syrup. Peel, quarter and core the apples, slice each in half. Add to the syrup, cover and poach gently for 15-20 minutes until tender. Draw pan aside and leave un-covered until cool.

Carefully lift out apples into a dish, reboil syrup, add cran-berries ; simmer for 5 minutes, then pour over apples. Chill before serving.

This simple dish is delicious with a sharp fruit compote

Menu 5 Pork

Serves 4

Starter : Fish en coquille

Main course : Barbecued pork fillet, Fried rice

Dessert : Strawberry mille feuilles

Alternative starter : Cream of lettuce soup

Timetable

Order of work

Day before
Make the puff pastry, wrap in polythene and store in refrigerator. Make redcurrant glaze.
Make mayonnaise.

Morning
Roll out puff pastry, line on to a baking sheet and bake.
Cook the fish and flake when cold. (Or make soup and sieve. Fry croûtons.)
Dice and salt cucumber, drain it and keep in refrigerator.
Cut up pork fillet and set in marinade. Wash and prepare salad and lettuce for fish en coquille and keep wrapped in a cloth in the refrigerator.
(Chop the mint for the soup.)
Boil the rice, drain and cover.
Assemble ingredients and equipment for final cooking from 6.15 for dinner around 8 pm.

6.15 Whip cream, fill and glaze the mille feuilles.

6.30 Dish up and garnish fish en coquille.

6.45 Brown the pork, add onions to the pan, then the stock and simmer.
Fry rice.
Toss salad.

7.30 Take up pork, reduce sauce and add the tomatoes.
Dish up the pork, cover with foil and keep warm. (Heat soup, add liaison and warm croûtons.)

8.00 Serve first course.

Fish en coquille

1½ lb firm white fish steak (cod, or turbot)
cut lemon, or juice of ½ lemon
salt
½ cucumber
black pepper (ground from mill)
1 teaspoon chopped parsley, mint and chives (mixed)
½ teaspoon white wine vinegar
1 tablespoon boiling water
¼ pint thick mayonnaise
6 lettuce leaves
12 anchovy fillets

6 deep scallop shells

each shell with anchovy fillets.

1 *Flaking the poached fish ready to place on the lettuce and cucumber*
2 *Laying the anchovy fillets in a cross on the mayonnaise-coated fish*

Method

First wash the fish. If using cod, dry it well and rub the surface with a cut lemon, sprinkle with salt and leave in a cool place for 30-60 minutes ; if using turbot, soak it for 15-20 minutes in cold water with a little salt and lemon juice.

Wipe the fish and place it in a well buttered ovenproof dish, adding an extra squeeze of lemon juice, and cover with buttered paper ; poach in a moderate oven pre-set at 350°F or Mark 4. Allow 15-20 minutes, depending on the thickness of the fish.

Peel the cucumber and cut it into small dice, salt lightly and leave in a cool place for 30 minutes, then drain away any liquid. Season the cucumber with black pepper, add the herbs and sprinkle with the wine vinegar. Whisk the boiling water into the mayonnaise.

Place a lettuce leaf in each scallop shell and then a spoonful of prepared cucumber. When the fish is cold, remove the skin and bones, then carefully flake flesh with a fork ; spoon fish into the shells and coat with the mayonnaise. Decorate the top of

Barbecued pork fillet

1½-2 lb pork fillet
2 oz butter
1 large onion (chopped)
¼ pint stock
3 tomatoes (skinned, seeds
   removed and sliced)
chopped parsley

For marinade
2 tablespoons soy sauce
1 tablespoon Worcestershire sauce
4 tablespoons tomato ketchup
1 tablespoon bottled fruit sauce
1 tablespoon honey
1 teaspoon French mustard
salt and pepper
sugar (to taste)

Method
Cut the pork fillet across into
2-inch pieces. Melt one-third of
the butter in a flameproof dish,
add the sauces and seasonings

for the marinade and mix together. Put in the pork pieces
and turn them around so that
they are well coated ; leave them
to marinate for 30 minutes or
longer.

Heat a sauté pan, drop in the
rest of the butter and, while it
is still foaming, put in the pieces
of pork, drained from the marinade. Add onion and sauté
slowly with pork until coloured.
Pour in stock, cover pan and
simmer for 30-40 minutes.

Lift out the pork, dish up on a
hot serving dish and add marinade to the pan. Reduce it until
sticky, then add the sliced tomatoes ; cook them for 3-4 minutes, then spoon over the meat.
Sprinkle with chopped parsley.
Serve with fried rice and salad
in season.

*Adding tomato slices to the reduced
marinade before spooning it over
pork*

Fried rice

8 oz long grain rice
1-2 tablespoons olive oil
1 small onion (chopped, or sliced)
salt and pepper
1 dessertspoon soy sauce
2 eggs (beaten)

Method
Cook the rice in boiling salted
water for 12 minutes. Drain well.
Heat the oil, add the onion and
cook slowly until it is just soft.
Add the rice to the pan and fry
until it is beginning to brown,
turning it well and seasoning.
Then add the soy sauce to taste
and the beaten eggs. Continue
to cook the rice, stirring it all
the time until it is dry.

Strawberry mille feuilles

1 lb strawberries
6 oz quantity of puff pastry
4 tablespoons almonds (browned and finely chopped)
$\frac{1}{2}$ pint double cream
1 teaspoon caster sugar
2-3 drops of vanilla essence
redcurrant glaze

Method

Set the oven at 425°F or Mark 7. Roll out the pastry as thinly as possible into a large sheet. Lay this over a dampened baking sheet, allowing the pastry to come slightly over the edge.

Prick the pastry well all over with a fork, then chill it for 5-10 minutes. Bake pastry in pre-set hot oven for 10-15 minutes ; when it is a good brown colour, slip a palette knife under it and turn it over. Replace pastry in the oven for a further 5 minutes, then slide it on to a wire rack to cool.

When cold, trim around the pastry edges, reserving the trimmings, and cut it into three strips 3-4 inches wide. Crush pastry trimmings and mix with the almonds. Whip the cream, sweeten with the sugar and add the vanilla essence.

Hull the strawberries, slice one-third, mix these with half the cream and spread over the first layer of pastry. Place a second layer of pastry on top,

1 Placing the second layer of puff pastry on the cream and strawberry mixture
2 Covering the bottom layer of the mille feuilles with a mixture made of crushed pastry trimmings and almonds

spread with the remaining cream and cover with the last piece of pastry. Brush the pastry top with redcurrant glaze.

Watchpoint The glaze must not be hot or else the cream will melt.

Arrange the remaining strawberries, halved, to cover, brush again with glaze. Cover the sides of the bottom layer only with chopped nuts and trimmings mixture.

Cream of lettuce soup

2 large lettuces
1 oz butter
1 medium-size onion (finely chopped)
1 rounded tablespoon plain flour
1½ pints milk
salt and pepper
mint (freshly chopped)
2 slices of bread (for fried croûtons)

For liaison
2 egg yolks, or 1 teaspoon arrowroot mixed with 2-3 tablespoons double cream

Any type of lettuce — round or Cos — is suitable for this soup and it is an excellent way to use lettuces that have 'bolted'.

Method

Wash the lettuce thoroughly, then shred it finely. Melt the butter in a pan, add the lettuce and onion, cover with a buttered paper and the lid of the pan and cook very gently for 8-10 minutes. Remove pan from heat and stir in the flour. Scald the milk, blend with the lettuce mixture and season ; stir until boiling, then leave to simmer very gently, with the lid half off the pan, for 10-15 minutes. Pass liquid through a Mouli sieve or blend in a liquidiser.

Return liquid to the rinsed-out pan, reheat to boiling point before adding liaison.

Watchpoint If using egg for the liaison, work the yolks and cream together with a wooden spoon and add 2 tablespoons of the hot soup ; return this mixture very slowly (in a thin steady stream) to the pan of soup and reheat carefully. If using the arrowroot mixed with cream, stir it briskly into the hot soup and reboil. Taste for seasoning.

Pour soup into a hot tureen and sprinkle with the chopped mint. Serve the fried croûtons separately.

Menu 6 Pork

Starter : Sole bonne femme

Main course : Stuffed pork fillets, Parsnip croquettes

Dessert : Rum pie

Alternative dessert : Stuffed apples in meringue with chocolate sauce

TIMETABLE

Order of work

Day before
Make shortcrust pastry and bake flan case.
(Prepare chocolate sauce ready for reheating. Make mincemeat. Poach apples, drain and stuff.)
Make hollandaise sauce for fish.
Make breadcrumbs for stuffing.

Morning
Cook apricots and sieve ; make sugar syrup for sauce. Prepare stuffing and leave pork ready for cooking. Prepare sprouts, potatoes and parsnips. Wash and slice mushrooms for fish dish and put in pan ready for cooking. Wash and dry fish and place in buttered dish ready for cooking.

Assemble ingredients and equipment for final cooking from 5.15 for dinner around 8 pm.

5.15 Set oven at 350°F or Mark 4.
Brown pork, put in oven.
Make filling for rum pie, put in the flan case and put in refrigerator to set.

5.45 Boil parsnips, keep warm.

6.30 Put fish to cook, on bottom shelf.

6.50 Make fish sauce and cook mushrooms.

7.00 Dish up fish, keep in warming drawer.
Cook sprouts and refresh.
Finish off rum pie and chill.
(Make meringue, cover apples and put in oven. Turn oven to 300°F or Mark 2.)

7.30 Take up pork, put in serving dish and make gravy.
Fry parsnip croquettes and keep warm.
Turn gas oven to lowest setting, electric oven off. Put plates and dishes to warm.

8.00 Glaze fish under grill and serve.

Sole bonne femme

4 **double, or 8 single, fillets of Dover, or lemon, sole**
6 **peppercorns**
1 **slice of onion**
1 **bayleaf**
1 **wineglass white wine**
1 **wineglass water**
2 **oz mushrooms (trimmed, washed and sliced)**
squeeze of lemon juice

For hollandaise sauce
1 **onion (sliced)**
2 **tablespoons tarragon vinegar**
1 **egg yolk (beaten)**
2 **oz butter**

For white wine sauce
1 **oz butter**
1 **rounded tablespoon plain flour**
$7\frac{1}{2}$ **fl oz fish stock (using white wine, see method)**
5 **tablespoons top of the milk**
salt and pepper

Method

First prepare the hollandaise sauce : add sliced onion to vinegar and reduce to 1 teaspoon over gentle heat. Strain on to the beaten yolk, standing bowl in a bain-marie ; add $\frac{1}{4}$ oz butter and beat until thick. Then add the rest of the butter slowly, beating well. When the consistency is of thick cream, cover and set aside.

Set oven at 350°F or Mark 4.

To prepare the sole : skin, wash and dry the fillets, fold in half lengthways, put in a buttered ovenproof dish, add peppercorns, onion slice and bayleaf, pour over the white wine and water. Cover with buttered paper and poach in pre-set oven for 15-20 minutes. Strain the liquid from the fish and measure it — there should be about $7\frac{1}{2}$ fl oz of stock.

To make white wine sauce : melt the butter in a saucepan, add the flour — off the heat — then pour on the fish stock. Stir until thick, add milk and bring quickly to the boil. Adjust seasoning and simmer sauce for 2-3 minutes to a coating consistency.

Cook mushrooms quickly in 1 tablespoon of water and a squeeze of lemon juice. Put fillets on serving dish, coat with the white wine sauce, scatter on the mushrooms and then put a tablespoon of the hollandaise on each fillet. Glaze under the grill and serve sole at once.

1 *Straining vinegar on to beaten egg yolk in the initial stages of hollandaise sauce*
2 *After butter is beaten into the egg yolk and vinegar the hollandaise sauce should have the consistency of thick cream*

Pouring white wine over fillets of sole, which have been folded in half lengthways

Putting hollandaise sauce on sole and mushrooms after coating with white sauce

Stuffed pork fillet

3-4 pork fillets (total weight
   1¾-2 lb)
1 oz butter
1 glass (2½ fl oz) sherry, or stock
1 tablespoon plain flour
½ pint stock
salt and pepper

For stuffing
2 oz butter
1 medium-size onion (finely
   chopped)
8 oz minced veal
1 dessertspoon chopped parsley
1 teaspoon mixed herbs
1 teaspoon sage
grated rind and juice of ½ lemon
1 cup fresh white breadcrumbs
salt and pepper
1 egg (beaten)

1 *Layering stuffing between beaten pork fillets*
2 *Browning shaped fillets before putting in oven with sherry or stock*

Method

Split the fillets two-thirds of the way through and beat with a heavy knife to flatten — many butchers sell the pork fillet cut and dressed in this way.

Set oven at 350°F or Mark 4.

To prepare stuffing : cook the onion in the butter until soft but not coloured, add to the other ingredients in a bowl and add enough beaten egg to bind. Layer this stuffing between the fillets, shaping them to form a loaf ; tie up with fine string or secure with poultry pins. Heat the butter in a flameproof casserole, or stewpan, and brown the pork carefully on both sides. Pour over the sherry (or stock), cover with greaseproof paper and lid, and cook in the pre-set oven for 2 hours.

Take up the meat and keep warm while preparing the gravy. Blend the flour into the butter and juices in the pan and cook slowly until russet-brown, tip in the stock and stir until boiling. Season with salt and pepper, simmer for 2-3 minutes and strain. Remove the string or

skewers from the pork and serve whole or sliced. Spoon a little gravy round and pour rest into a sauce boat.

Parsnip croquettes

2 **large parsnips**
a **little beaten egg**
3 **tablespoons dried white breadcrumbs**
2 **oz butter (for frying)**

Method

Cut the parsnips in finger length pieces (about 3 inches long by $\frac{3}{4}$ inch thick) and cook in slated water until tender (about 15 minutes) ; drain and return to pan, with $\frac{1}{2}$ oz of the butter, on a low heat to dry. Turn on to a plate to cool. Brush the parsnip pieces with the beaten egg and coat with the crumbs. Fry croquettes in hot butter until golden-brown.

Rum pie

For rich shortcrust pastry
6 oz plain flour
3 oz butter
1 oz shortening
1 tablespoon caster sugar
1 egg yolk
1-2 tablespoons water

For filling
8 fl oz milk
$\frac{1}{4}$ nutmeg (grated)
2 eggs (separated)
3 oz caster sugar
pinch of salt
1 teaspoon gelatine (soaked in 3
  teaspoons cold water)
$\frac{1}{8}$ pint rum

To finish
1 oz plain block chocolate
1 tablespoon water
$\frac{1}{4}$ pint double cream
1 teaspoon rum
1 dessertspoon caster sugar

7-8 inch diameter flan ring

Method

Prepare the shortcrust pastry. Line the flan ring with it and bake blind for 20-25 minutes, then set aside to cool.

To prepare the filling : scald the milk with the nutmeg. Beat the egg yolks, sugar and salt together until thick and light in colour, pour on the hot milk and cook in a double saucepan until the mixture coats the back of a spoon. Stir in the soaked gelatine and allow to cool. When the mixture begins to thicken, stir in the rum and finally, the stiffly whisked egg whites. Pour into the prepared pastry case and put in the refrigerator to set.

Melt the chocolate in the water, set pan aside and allow it to cool. Whip the cream and divide in half. Flavour half with the rum and the other half with the sugar. Mix the rum-flavoured cream with the cold, melted chocolate, cover the top of the pie with the sugared cream and then coat this with the chocolate cream. Chill again in the refrigerator before serving.

Adding the melted chocolate to the rum-flavoured whipped cream

Rum pie — a shortcrust pastry flan case with a rum-flavoured custard filling. The topping is a rum-flavoured chocolate cream on top of a layer of sugared, whipped cream

Stuffed apples
in meringue with chocolate sauce

6 large dessert apples
3 tablespoons granulated sugar
(dissolved in ¾ pint water)
1 vanilla pod, or 3-4 drops of
vanilla essence

For mincemeat mixture
4 oz mixed dried fruit
small piece of candied peel
½ oz butter

For meringue
2 egg whites
4 oz caster sugar

For chocolate sauce
2 tablespoons cocoa
1 tablespoon caster sugar

Method

Bring sugar syrup to boil and boil steadily for 10 minutes, flavouring with vanilla. Peel and core apples (a pippin variety such as Cox's or Blenheim is ideal) and poach them carefully in the syrup. To make sure that apples are tender right through, turn them during the cooking time. When tender, remove from the pan with a draining spoon (reserving the syrup) and arrange in an ovenproof serving dish.

To prepare the mincemeat : chop the fruit and candied peel and put into a pan with the butter and 1 tablespoon of the syrup in which the apples were cooked. Stir over a gentle heat for 5 minutes, then stuff the mincemeat into the cooked apples. Set oven at 275-300°F or Mark 1-2.

To prepare the meringue : whip the egg whites until stiff, then whisk in 1 tablespoon of the sugar for 1 minute and, using a tablespoon, fold in the remainder carefully. Cover each apple with meringue. This can be done with a spoon, or piped on with a vegetable rose pipe. Dust with caster sugar and bake in pre-set oven for 15-20 minutes until golden-brown.

To make chocolate sauce : mix cocoa and sugar to a paste with a little of the poaching syrup, add mixture to pan of syrup and simmer gently for 15 minutes. Pour hot sauce round apples before serving.

Meringue is spooned or piped on to the cooked apple and then baked. Chocolate sauce is poured over apples before serving

Menu 7 Lamb

Starter : Game soup

Main course : Roast saddle of lamb jardinière, Roast
potatoes, Jardinière platter

Dessert : Oranges en surprise

Petits fours

TIMETABLE

Order of work

Day before
Make stock for the game
soup and keep in a cool
place.
Make the petits fours and
store in an airtight tin.

Morning
Make game soup but do not
add liaison.
Prepare and trim all the
vegetables for the jardinière
platter.
Peel potatoes and leave in
cold water.
Scoop out oranges and
macerate glacé fruits.

Assemble equipment and
ingredients for final cooking
from 5.30 for dinner around
8 pm.

5.30 Set oven at 400°F or
Mark 6.
Make meringue for
oranges, complete and
dish up.

5.50 Prepare saddle of lamb
and put in oven.

6.15 Cook carrots and
artichokes.

6.45 Put potatoes to roast
around the joint.

7.00 Cook cauliflower and
onions.

7.15 Cook the sprouts,
courgettes (if using) and
mushrooms.

7.30 Take up saddle of lamb,
make gravy and dish up
vegetables ; keep them
hot.
Add liaison to the soup.

8.00 Serve first course.

Game soup

carcass of 1 pheasant, or 2 grouse
  (cooked)
1 large onion (stuck with a clove)
1 clove of garlic (unpeeled)
4 carrots (peeled and quartered)
1 turnip (peeled and quartered)
bouquet garni (containing a stick
  of celery)
9 peppercorns
pinch of salt
6 pints brown stock
4-6 oz cold cooked game meat
2-3 oz fresh white breadcrumbs
pinch of ground mace
1 glass golden sherry
¼ pint double cream
3 egg yolks
croûtons of fried bread

Method

Cut the carcass into small pieces with kitchen or game scissors and put into a large pan with the vegetables, bouquet garni, peppercorns, salt and the brown stock. Cover pan and simmer gently for 2-3 hours until stock is well flavoured and reduced to about half its quantity ; strain.

Chop the game meat quite finely and mix with the breadcrumbs, moistened with about ½ pint stock, and pound or work in the liquidiser to a smooth paste or panade. Dilute this mixture with the rest of the stock, return it to the rinsed-out pan, season, add the mace and bring to the boil. Then add the sherry.

Beat the cream into the egg yolks with a wooden spoon, add 2-3 tablespoons of the hot soup to this liaison, mix well and then return to the soup very slowly, stirring all the time. Reheat soup carefully without boiling and serve with croûtons of fried bread.

Cream, sherry and fried croûtons are added to game soup before serving

Roast saddle of lamb jardinière

Main course

1 saddle of lamb (8-10 lb)
2 oz butter
pepper (ground from mill)
2 wineglasses white wine
$\frac{1}{4}$ pint brown stock (a little extra
   may be needed for roasting)

For gravy
1 tablespoon plain flour
$\frac{1}{2}$ pint brown stock

Method

Weigh the lamb and allow 15-20 minutes cooking time per lb. Set the oven at 400°F or Mark 6. Spread the joint liberally with the butter and season with pepper ; pour over the white wine and stock and put joint in the pre-set hot oven. Baste joint every 15-20 minutes. Add a little extra stock if the liquid in the tin reduces too much.

At the end of the cooking time, remove the joint from the roasting tin and keep hot ; make gravy from the juices in the pan. To do this, spoon or tip off the fat from the pan very carefully, leaving all the sediment behind, and add 1 tablespoon flour to this. Cook it slowly until well coloured. Tip on the extra $\frac{1}{2}$ pint stock, stir until boiling then simmer until gravy is well reduced and has a good flavour. Strain it into a sauce boat for serving.

Carve the saddle in slices almost down to the bone, first running knife around and under meat, and place on a serving dish. (This will make serving at the table much easier).) Serve with roast potatoes, and a jardinière platter.

Jardinière platter

$1\frac{1}{2}$ lb carrots
$1\frac{1}{2}$ lb small brussels sprouts
   (trimmed)
1 lb small pickling onions (skinned)
2 lb jerusalem artichokes (peeled),
   or 1 lb courgettes
$\frac{1}{2}$ lb button mushrooms
2 cauliflowers

For serving
1 teaspoon granulated sugar (for
   carrots)
teaspoon chopped mint (for carrots)
$3\frac{3}{4}$ oz butter
2 teaspoons granulated sugar
   (for onions)
juice of $\frac{1}{2}$ small lemon
salt and pepper
1 dessertspoon chopped parsley

The vegetables are all cooked separately and then arranged together on a large serving platter.

Method

Carrots
Peel and quarter lengthwise. Cover with cold water and add 1 teaspoon sugar, a pinch of salt, $\frac{1}{2}$ oz butter, and cook until tender and all the water has evaporated (about 15 minutes). Add 1 teaspoon chopped mint before serving.

Brussels sprouts
Cook until just tender in boiling, salted water for about 8 minutes, drain and toss in $\frac{1}{4}$ oz butter.

Roast saddle of lamb jardinière

Pickling onions

Cover with cold water and bring to the boil — drain well. Return to the pan with 1 oz butter, 2 teaspoons sugar ; cover and cook slowly until they are brown and sticky. Shake the pan from time to time and turn the onions. They should be tender after 8-10 minutes, but this does depend on the speed of cooking

Jerusalem artichokes

Cut into even-size pieces after peeling and cook in boiling salted water with a slice of lemon to help keep their colour and to give flavour. When tender, drain artichokes well and add $\frac{1}{2}$ oz butter to the pan with pepper ground from the mill and a little extra salt to season.

Courgettes

Thickly slice and blanch the courgettes in boiling water for 1 minute. Drain and return to the pan with $\frac{1}{2}$ oz butter, cover pan tightly and cook until tender for about 8-10 minutes.

Mushrooms

Wash and trim the mushrooms and put them on a well buttered ovenproof plate. Season with salt and pepper and a squeeze of lemon juice, cover with a buttered paper and a pan lid or a second ovenproof plate and cook for about 10 minutes on the shelf under the meat in the oven.

Cauliflower

Divide the cauliflower into sprigs and, using a potato peeler, remove the outside skin on the stalk of the cauliflower sprigs. Cook in boiling salted water until just tender (about 5 minutes) and drain well.

To dish up, arrange the vegetables in rows in a large hot serving platter. Melt $1\frac{1}{2}$ oz butter in a small pan and cook slowly until a nut-brown, add the lemon juice, salt and pepper and the chopped parsley. Pour this butter, while it is still foaming, over the vegetables, particularly the artichokes (or courgettes) and the cauliflower.

Roast potatoes

Choose medium to large potatoes of even size. Peel and blanch by putting into cold salted water and bringing to the boil. Drain thoroughly and lightly scratch the surface with a fork (this will prevent a dry and leathery exterior after cooking). Now put the potatoes into smoking hot fat in the same tin as the meat, 40-45 minutes before the meat is fully cooked, and baste well. Cook until soft (test by piercing with a cooking fork or fine skewer), basting them when you baste the meat and turning after 25 minutes. Drain well on kitchen paper, pile in a vegetable dish and sprinkle with a little salt. Do not cover before serving.

Oranges en surprise

12 large seedless oranges
6 oz glacé fruit
6 tablespoons Grand Marnier
4 egg quantity of meringue cuite
caster sugar (for dusting)

Any glacé fruit — including stem ginger, angelica and cherries — can be used. The liqueur can be omitted, but it does give a good flavour.

Method

Set the oven at 400°F or Mark 6. Slice or dice the glacé fruit and macerate pieces in the Grand Marnier. Slice off the flower end of the oranges and, using a grapefruit knife, scoop out the flesh. Take out the core, and remove as many membranes as possible. Mix the orange flesh with the glacé fruit and replace in the skins. Have ready the meringue and pipe this on each orange ; place them in a roasting tin containing ice cubes. Dust with sugar and put into the pre-set hot oven until just coloured (5-10 minutes), then take out and serve cool.

Watchpoint The meringue should be browned quickly because if the oranges are allowed to cook in any way they will get a marmalade taste. The ice cubes in the roasting tin help to keep the oranges from cooking.

1 *Putting a mixture of orange flesh and glacé fruit into one of the scooped-out oranges for oranges en surprise*
2 *Piping on meringue before placing oranges in a tin of ice to stop them cooking while meringue is browning*

Petits fours

These petits fours are all made from the same foundation : an almond and meringue paste, butter cream and fondant icing.

Basic foundation

For almond and meringue paste
4 egg whites
4¼ oz ground almonds
4¼ oz caster sugar
1¾ oz plain flour

For butter cream
3 oz caster sugar
3 egg yolks
6 oz unsalted butter
1 lb fondant icing

Forcing bag, ¼-inch diameter éclair pipe, a rose pipe, and a plain pipe

Method
Set the oven at 375°F or Mark 5. Whip the egg whites until stiff and firm. Sieve the almonds, sugar and flour together and fold into the egg whites, using a metal spoon.

Put the mixture into the forcing bag, fitted with the éclair pipe, and pipe the paste on to a buttered and floured baking sheet as follows :

For **Columbines** and **Sultanes** : shape two thirds of the paste into small rounds like small macaroons.

For **Clemences** shape rest of the paste into small langues de chats biscuits.

Bake these petits fours in the pre-set moderately hot oven for 7-8 minutes and then leave them to cool.

To make the butter cream : dissolve the sugar in 3-4 fl oz water over gentle heat, then boil steadily to the thread stage (216-218°F). Pour the syrup while still hot on to egg yolks, whisk until a thick mousse is formed. Cream the butter until soft and beat in the eggs and sugar mousse a little at a time. Flavour and finish petits fours as given in the following recipes.

Columbines

Take half of the small macaroon shapes and pipe a kirsch flavoured butter cream in a pyramid on top of each one, then place a tiny piece of glacé cherry on top of each pyramid. Chill well, then ice with a thin, kirsch flavoured fondant so that the cherry can be seen through it.

Sultanes

Using the remaining small macaroons, pipe butter cream (flavoured with coffee and pounded praline) around the edge of each one, leaving the centre uncovered ; chill them well. Then coat the rounds with coffee fondant icing ; when it is set, place a little quince or redcurrant jelly in the middle of each one.

Clemences

Take the small langues de chats biscuits ; cover each one with coffee-flavoured butter cream, using éclair pipe, then chill well. Then cover with coffee fondant icing and place a piece of shredded browned almond in the centre of each one.

Menu 8 Lamb

Starter : Brill with cucumber

Main course : Braised stuffed leg of lamb, Brussels sprout cream,
Château potatoes

Dessert : Mincemeat flan de luxe

Alternative starter : Chicken or turkey broth

TIMETABLE

Day before
Make the mincemeat.
Make the shortcrust pastry
and chill.
Prepare stock for the braise
(and soup).

Morning
Prepare fish and put in dish
for cooking ; cut and blanch
cucumber and put in pan
with butter (or make soup
but do not add cream or
parsley).
Prepare brussels sprout
cream and leave in cake tin
ready for cooking.
Stuff and lard the meat.
Cut vegetables for braised
leg of lamb, and make sauce.
Line and fill flan, leave ready
for baking.

Order of work
4.50 Set oven at 350°F or
Mark 4.
Start to cook lamb and
transfer casserole to oven.

5.20 Put flan into oven on top
shelf. Brown potatoes,
drain off fat ; set aside.
Whip and flavour
cream for flan, cover,

keep in cool place.

6.00 Take out flan and cool.

6.45 Put sprout cream into
oven by meat. Put potatoes
at top of oven.
Put the fish
into oven under meat.

7.10 Take meat from oven,
strain off liquid, put meat
back in oven to keep hot.
Finish sauce and
keep hot. Take fish out,
make fish sauce and keep
both warm. Turn oven to
lowest setting. Put serv-
ing dishes to warm.
Simmer cucumber in
butter on top of stove.

7.30 Turn sprout cream on to
serving dish but do not lift
off mould ; keep hot.

7.50 Put sauce and cheese on
fish, glaze under grill
(or heat soup). Garnish
starter (or soup) and serve.
Slip flan into oven
to heat through.
Add whipped cream
just before serving.

Brill with cucumber

4-6 fillets of brill (1½-2 lb)
rind and juice of ½ lemon
¼ pint water
salt
peppercorns
1 large cucumber
½ oz butter
dill, or mint, or parsley (chopped)
1 dessertspoon grated cheese

For sauce
1 oz butter
1 rounded tablespoon plain flour
¼ pint milk
salt and pepper

Method

Wash, skin and dry fillets. Fold the ends of the fillets under, put in a buttered flameproof dish, pour on the lemon juice and water and grate over a little lemon rind. Season with salt and a few peppercorns, cover with buttered greaseproof paper and poach in the oven at 325°F or Mark 3 for 15-20 minutes, or until tender. Strain the fish and reserve the liquor.

Peel cucumber, cut into chunks and drop into boiling salted water for 1 minute then drain. Melt a good ½ oz butter, add the cucumber and season to taste. Cover and simmer until almost tender (about 5 minutes). Add the dill, mint or parsley.

To make sauce : melt the butter in another pan, remove from heat, blend in the flour and the strained liquor from the fish. Stir the sauce over gentle heat until thickening, then add milk. Bring to the boil and reduce rapidly to the consistency of cream. Taste for seasoning.

Dish up the fish, pour over the sauce, sprinkle with the cheese and brown lightly under the grill. Garnish with the cucumber.

Brill is a fish that may be overlooked by some people; however, it makes a good dish when served with white sauce and cucumber

Braised stuffed leg of lamb

1 small leg of lamb (about 3½ lb)
8 anchovy fillets
3 tablespoons milk (for soaking anchovy)
8 oz cooked gammon (sliced)
1 shallot (finely chopped)
1 teaspoon chopped parsley
pinch of thyme, or marjoram (chopped)

For braising
2 carrots
2 onions
2-3 sticks of celery
1-2 tablespoons oil
2 cloves of garlic (not peeled)
1 wineglass red wine (optional)
½ pint jellied brown bone stock
bouquet garni

For sauce
1 oz butter
2 shallots (finely chopped)
1 tablespoon plain flour
1 large teaspoon tomato purée
¾ pint jellied bone stock

To stuff the boned leg of lamb, first place anchovy fillets on gammon slices, sprinkle with shallot and herbs. Roll up, open up meat and insert gammon

Method

Ask your butcher to bone the leg of lamb without cutting the skin. Soak half the anchovies in a little milk to remove excess salt. Lay the gammon slices overlapping on a board, drain the anchovy fillets and place on top. Sprinkle well with the shallot and herbs and roll up to form a tube. Push this into boned lamb and tie up securely.

Lard the meat with the remaining anchovies, ie. sew them into the meat with a larding needle. Dice the vegetables for braising. Heat the oil in a heavy cast iron casserole, brown the meat lightly on all sides, then take out of the pan. Add the vegetables, cover pan and reduce heat to cook gently for 8-10 minutes until they have taken colour and absorbed the fat. Place the leg of lamb on the vegetables, add the garlic and wine and flame it (heat and set it alight to burn out alcohol), then add the stock; tuck the bouquet garni alongside and bring to the boil. Cover the pan and cook meat in the oven pre-set 350°F or Mark 4, for 2 hours.

To prepare the sauce: melt the butter in a pan, add the

shallot, cook slowly until soft, then stir in the flour and brown slowly. Stir in the tomato purée and stock, bring to the boil and simmer for 30-40 minutes.

Take cooked meat from oven, strain off the liquid and boil to reduce to half the quantity. Add this to the sauce.

Remove the strings from the meat, place it on a serving dish and pour over a little of the sauce. Pour the rest into a sauceboat and serve separately.

Serve with château potatoes (see page 147) and brussels sprout cream.

Brussels sprout cream

2 lb brussels sprouts
½ teacup hot milk
1 teacup fresh white bread crumbs
1½ oz butter
1 egg yolk
grated nutmeg (to taste)
salt and pepper

6-inch diameter cake tin, or ring mould

Method
Wash and trim the sprouts, cook for 8-10 minutes, until tender, in plenty of boiling salted water, then drain and rinse well in cold water. Drain again and press to remove any excess water. Pass through a Mouli sieve. Pour the hot milk on to the breadcrumbs in a bowl and leave to soak.

Put the sprout purée in a pan, add the butter, a small piece at a time, and stir over heat until the purée leaves the side of the pan. Draw aside, add soaked crumbs, egg yolk, nutmeg and season well. Put purée into buttered tin or ring mould, cover with greaseproof paper and stand in a roasting tin half filled with hot water in the oven. Cook in the oven at 350°F or Mark 4 for 40 minutes. Leave for a few minutes before turning out of the cake tin or mould.

The cream can be left quite plain or coated with a white or cheese sauce — ½ pint would be sufficient.

Mincemeat flan de luxe

For rich shortcrust pastry
8 oz plain flour
salt
4 oz butter
2 oz lard
1 dessertspoon caster sugar
1 egg yolk
2-3 tablespoons water

For fresh mincemeat
8 oz Cox's apples (weight when
   peeled and cored) — chopped
1 oz orange candied peel (chopped)
8 oz raisins
8 oz currants
4 oz sultanas
6 oz grapes (peeled and pipped)
2 rounded tablespoons almonds
   (blanched and schredded)
grated rind and juice of 1 small
   lemon
pinch of mixed spice
6 oz brown sugar
1 oz melted butter
1 small glass brandy, or sherry

To decorate
2-3 tablespoons whipped cream
little rum, or brandy

*8-inch diameter flan ring ; 3-inch
   diameter plain cutter*

Only half this quantity of mincemeat is needed to fill the 8-
inch flan ring. The remainder
will keep up to 2 weeks in sealed
jars (see method).

Method

To prepare pastry : sift the flour
and salt together, cut butter and
lard into flour until well coated
and in small pieces. Rub in fats
until mixture resembles fine
breadcrumbs. Stir in sugar, mix
egg yolk and water, add to the
dry ingredients and mix quickly
to a firm dough.

Knead pastry lightly on a
floured board until smooth.
Chill slightly before use.

To prepare mincemeat : dried
fruit should be washed and
dried, candied peel well soaked
in water to soften. Chop
apples and candied peel separately, then mix with the other
ingredients. If the grapes are
large, cut them into 2-3 pieces.

When mincemeat is well
mixed, set aside quantity to be
used immediately and fill remainder into jars. Cover with
circle of greaseproof paper and
cellophane, then tie down or
secure with an elastic band.

Set the flan ring on a baking
sheet. Set oven at 375°F or
Mark 5.

Use three-quarters of the
pastry to line the flan ring. Fill
with mincemeat. Roll out the
remaining pastry and cut a
circle the same size as the flan
ring. Stamp out a hole in the
middle with a plain cutter. Put
this pastry ring on top of the
flan, crimp round the edge to
decorate and seal in, brush with
water and sprinkle with sugar.
Bake in the pre-set oven for 30-
40 minutes.

Just before serving pile 2-3
tablespoons of whipped cream,
lightly flavoured with rum or
brandy, in the middle of the flan.

After lining flan ring with three-quarters of the pastry, the mincemeat is spooned in. A hole is cut out of the middle of the remaining pastry, which is then laid over top of flan ; edges are crimped to seal and to decorate

Chicken or turkey broth

2 pints strong chicken, or turkey,
  stock
3 tablespoons carrot (finely diced)
  — discard centre yellow core
2 tablespoons finely chopped
  onion
2 tablespoons long grain rice
salt and pepper
3 tablespoons double cream
1 dessertspoon chopped parsley

Method
Prepare stock from carcass
bones by adding enough water
just to cover. For a strong, clear
stock, simmer it gently, do not
boil hard. Strain and leave to
cool ; remove all fat.

Put the stock, vegetables and
rice in a pan, season, cover and
simmer for 30-40 minutes. Taste
for seasoning. Stir in cream,
sprinkle with chopped parsley
and serve.

*A chicken or turkey can serve you
well. Not only do you get tender
meat, but also a very wholesome
broth can be made from the carcass.
So these birds are very economical
buys because there's little wastage.
After broth is made, add some
cream to each bowl and sprinkle
over a little chopped parsley*

Menu 9 Lamb

Starter : Potage madrilène

Main course : Loin of lamb portugaise, Courgettes aux
fines herbes, Château potatoes

Dessert : Crème brûlée

Alternative starter : Grilled grapefruit

TIMETABLE

Order of work

Day before
Prepare crème brûlée and
put it aside ready for final
grilling.
Make stuffing for the lamb.
Make chicken stock for soup
and chill.

Morning
Grill crème brûlée ; pick over
and sugar the accompanying
fruit.
Bone and stuff lamb ; make
stock.
Make soup and strain.
Do preliminary preparation of
the vegetables.
Assemble ingredients and
equipment for final cooking
from 5.50 for dinner around
8 pm.

5.50 Set oven at 400°F or
Mark 6.

6.00 Put in the lamb.
(Cut grapefruit and
sprinkle with sherry).

6.20 Baste lamb.

6.40 Turn meat, remove
buttered paper and baste
again.

7.00 Make lemon sauce for
lamb.
Take up the lamb and
keep it warm.
Start cooking the potatoes
and courgettes ; put them
in the oven to keep warm
when they are done.

7.30 Carve the lamb.
Reheat soup.

7.55 (Sugar and grill grapefruit).

8.00 Serve first course.

Potage madrilène

Starter

- 2 pints chicken stock (cold)
- 1 medium-size onion (finely chopped)
- 1 oz butter
- 1 large can (1 lb 12 oz) Italian plum tomatoes
- bouquet garni (containing a strip of lemon rind)
- salt (to taste)
- 6 black peppercorns (to taste)
- 5 fl oz sherry
- 1 tablespoon arrowroot (slaked with 2 tablespoons water)
- squeeze of lemon juice
- 1 small carton (2½ fl oz) single cream
- 1 tablespoon snipped chives

Method

Skim the stock thoroughly. Cook the onion slowly in butter in a pan until soft but not coloured, add stock, tomatoes, bouquet garni and peppercorns. Stir until boiling, crushing tomatoes with wooden spoon, cover and simmer for 40 minutes. Pass through a Mouli sieve or rub through a nylon strainer.

Watchpoint These methods are better than using an electric blender, as the latter breaks down the seeds. Both flavour and appearance are improved if the seeds are removed by straining.

Return the soup to the rinsed-out pan, boil the sherry until reduced to half and add to soup. Thicken very slightly with the arrowroot — this is done just to bind in the small amount of butter and to give a certain smoothness on the palate. Reboil, add lemon juice and adjust the seasoning.

A spoonful of cream should be floated on top of each soup cup or plate as it is served; sprinkle with fresh snipped chives.

Loin of lamb portugaise   Main course

2½-3 lb loin of lamb (chined)
1½ pints water
1 tablespoon instant browned
   onions
1 carrot
bouquet garni
salt and pepper
1-2 oz butter
1 wineglass white wine

For stuffing
4 oz walnut kernels
1 medium-size onion (finely
   chopped)
1½ oz butter
½ cup (1½ oz) fresh white breadcrumbs
1 tablespoon chopped parsley
1 teaspoon marjoram
grated rind and juice of ½ lemon
1 egg (beaten)

For lemon sauce
1 oz butter
1 rounded tablespoon plain flour
½ pint stock
1 tablespoon redcurrant jelly
juice of ½ lemon and ½ orange
1 tablespoon chopped mint

Method

First make the stock : remove the chine bone and any small chop bones from the lamb and put these in a pan with the water, onion, carrot, bouquet garni and seasoning and simmer for 45-50 minutes ; strain and then reduce the liquid to ½ pint.

To prepare the stuffing : grind the walnuts through a small mill or mincer. Cook the onion in the butter until soft and golden, then add with the nuts to the breadcrumbs and herbs. Mix in the lemon rind and juice and add just enough egg to bind. Season well.

Spread the lamb with the stuffing, roll up and secure with poultry pins and fine string (or sew up using fine string and a trussing needle). Score the surface of the lamb and rub with the butter and set in a roasting tin ; pour round the wine, cover with a buttered paper and roast in the oven, pre-set at 400°F or Mark 6, for about 1¼ hours, basting from time to time. After 40 minutes, turn the meat and remove the buttered paper.

Meanwhile prepare the sauce : melt the butter, stir in the flour and cook slowly until russet-brown. Draw the pan aside, pour on the stock, add the redcurrant jelly and fruit juices and blend until smooth. Season well and stir over gentle heat until boiling, then keep the sauce simmering.

Take up the meat and keep it warm. Tip off the fat from the roasting tin and strain the remaining sediment into the sauce. Carve the meat and arrange it on a hot serving dish. Skim the

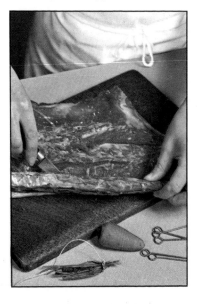

Remove chine bone and small chop bones from the lamb before stuffing ▶   75

Loin of lamb portugaise continued

sauce well and add the chopped mint ; spoon a little sauce over the meat to keep it moist and serve the rest in a sauce boat. Serve with château potatoes (see page 147) and courgettes aux fines herbes.

Courgettes aux fines herbes

1 lb courgettes
1-2 oz butter
salt and pepper
1 tablespoon chopped, fresh
   mixed herbs

Method

Wipe courgettes, trim ends and cut into $\frac{1}{2}$-inch slanting slices. Melt the butter in a sauté pan, add the courgettes, season and cover with a buttered paper and a lid.

Cook courgettes over gentle heat, shaking the pan occasionally to stop them from sticking, for 15-20 minutes. Add the chopped herbs, then turn them into a hot serving dish.

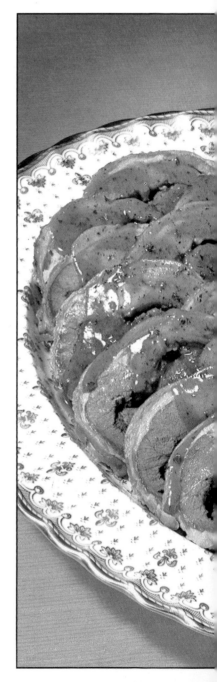

Loin of lamb portugaise, garnished with watercress. A little of the sauce is spooned over the meat and the rest is served separately. Courgettes aux fines herbes make an unusual accompaniment

Crème brûlée

1 pint double cream
1 vanilla pod (split)
4 egg yolks
4-5 tablespoons caster sugar

Method

Set the oven at 325°F or Mark 3. Put the cream and vanilla pod in the top of a double boiler, cover and bring to scalding point. Meanwhile work yolks and 1 tablespoon of the sugar with a wooden spoon until light in colour.

Remove vanilla pod and pour the cream on to the egg yolks and sugar and mix well ; return mixture to the pan and thicken very carefully over the heat, stirring continuously.

Watchpoint On no account allow the mixture to boil ; it has reached the right consistency when it coats a wooden spoon.

Strain the mixture into a shallow ovenproof dish and place in the pre-set oven for 5-8 minutes, until a skin forms on the top. Allow cream to stand in a cool place for several hours or preferably overnight.

Pre-heat grill. Dust top of cream evenly with remaining sugar and slip it under grill at least 4 inches away from the heat. At this distance the sugar has a chance to melt before it begins to brown and an even coating of caramel over the cream is ensured. Remove the cream from under the grill and let it stand in the refrigerator for 2-3 hours before serving. A bowl of sugared fruit — raspberries, strawberries or currants, or a mixed selection — may be served separately. This makes a good contrast to the rich cream.

The custard for crème brûlée is the right consistency when it coats a wooden spoon

Dessert

Crème brûlée, served with sugared raspberries, makes a cool, rich sweet

Grilled grapefruit

2 grapefruit
4 tablespoons sherry
4 dessertspoons soft light brown
sugar
1 oz butter ($\frac{1}{4}$ oz per person)

Method

Prepare the halved grapefruit in the following way. Using a small sharp knife, preferably with a curved and serrated blade, first cut out the core, then run the knife round the outside edge of the grapefruit, cutting between the flesh and the pith. Then slip knife either side of each membrane and lift out carefully without disturbing the segments of grapefruit ; with practice this is done very speedily and easily. Carefully remove any pips.

Sprinkle each half with the sherry and set in a dish ready for grilling. This can be done several hours before the meal.

Pre-heat grill, sprinkle sugar over the grapefruit halves and dot with butter ; cook until the sugar is lightly caramelised (browned but not burnt). Serve hot.

Before grilling grapefruit, remove the core and cut flesh away from the pith. Slip knife carefully down sides of membranes to separate each segment

Menu 10 Chicken

Starter : Stuffed apple salad, Cheese sablés

Main course : Chicken provençale, Saffron rice, Green salad

Dessert : Cold chocolate soufflé

TIMETABLE

Day before
Make and bake cheese
sablés : when cool store in
airtight container.

Morning
Joint chicken. Scald, skin
tomatoes, remove seeds
and chop flesh.
Make soufflé but do not
decorate.
Wash green salad ; prepare
French dressing and store
in a jar (or prepare French
beans). Wash and shred
celery and leave in bowl of
iced water.
Soak saffron.
Cook rice, and when dry
store in covered basin.
Fry bacon and crush. Cook
onion for saffron rice and
leave in the pan.

Assemble equipment for final
cooking from 6.30 for dinner
around 8 pm.

Order of work

6.30 Whip cream, grate
chocolate, and decorate
soufflé.
Prepare stuffed apple
salad, dish up and leave
in a cool place.

7.00 Start to brown chicken.
Put plates and serving
dishes to warm.
Put green salad in bowl
ready for tossing (or cook
French beans, drain and
refresh).

7.15 Turn chicken, add other
ingredients and cook until
tender.
Toss green salad.
Heat rice with saffron in
pan with onion and butter.
Take up chicken, trim
joints and arrange in
serving dish, cover with
foil. Boil tomato mixture
to reduce but do not pour
over chicken until just
before serving.
Season rice and add
bacon and dish up.
(Reheat French beans in
butter.)

8.00 Serve first course.

Stuffed apple salad

4 even-size apples
2 inner sticks from a head of celery
2 tablespoons cream
1 dessertspoon lemon juice, or
    wine vinegar
little caster sugar
black pepper (ground from mill)
garlic crushed with salt (optional)

To garnish
4 walnut halves

Method

Shred celery sticks very finely and place in a bowl of ice-cold water so that they curl.

Choose apples of a pippin variety with unblemished skins. Wipe and polish them with a soft cloth. Cut off tops and carefully scoop out the flesh without breaking the skin. Remove cores and seeds, chop the flesh and place in a bowl.

Drain and dry shredded celery. Add to the chopped apple and mix well.

Blend cream, lemon juice or wine vinegar, sugar and seasonings together and pour over the apple and celery. Stir carefully until fruit is well coated with dressing.

Watchpoint If the dressing is stirred vigorously, it will become too thick and may curdle.

Spoon mixture into apple cases and decorate each apple with a walnut half. Serve with cheese sablés.

Cheese sablés

3 oz cheese (grated)
3 oz plain flour (sifted)
3 oz butter
salt and pepper
1 egg (lightly beaten)

Sift flour into a bowl. Cut butter into flour with a palette knife and, as soon as pieces are well coated with flour, rub in with your fingertips until mixture resembles fine breadcrumbs.

Add cheese and season to taste. Press mixture together to make a dough. Flour, wrap dough in greaseproof paper, chill in refrigerator. Set oven at 375°F or Mark 5.

Carefully roll out pastry into a fairly thin oblong, flouring rolling pin well because this pastry tends to stick ; if it does, ease it free with a palette knife. Cut into strips about 2 inches wide. Brush with beaten egg and cut strips into triangles.

Place sablés on a baking sheet lined with greaseproof paper, and cook in the pre-set oven for 10 minutes until golden-brown.

Watchpoint Take baking sheet out of oven at once. Lift off greaseproof paper, with cooked sablés on it. Cheese scorches easily so that if you remove them from tray one by one, the last biscuits could become scorched through over-cooking.

Serve the sablés cold.

Chicken provençale

3 lb roasting chicken, or chicken
  joints
2 oz butter
4 cloves of garlic (unpeeled)
6 large tomatoes
1 wineglass sherry, or brandy
1 teaspoon tomato purée
salt and pepper
1 tablespoon mixed herbs
  (chopped)

Some aromatic herbs, such as marjoram, oregano, thyme or basil, can be used in this dish but they must be mixed with parsley in the proportion of one-third aromatic herbs to two-thirds parsley.

Method
If using a whole chicken, joint it.

Melt butter in a frying pan, add unpeeled garlic cloves and chicken joints, skin-side down, and cook slowly for about 15 minutes until joints are half cooked.

Meanwhile, scald and skin the tomatoes, remove seeds and chop flesh very finely.

Turn the chicken over at this half-cooked stage, remove garlic and pour in sherry or brandy. Set this alight and when the alcohol has burnt out, simmer until all the liquid has evaporated. The chicken should look brown and sticky at this stage. Add the tomato flesh, tomato purée and seasoning to the pan and continue cooking for about 15 minutes until chicken is tender and the tomatoes well reduced.

Remove chicken from pan, trim joints by cutting away any excess bone showing after the natural shrinkage of flesh has taken place during cooking and arrange in a serving dish.

Boil remaining tomato mixture to reduce further, then pour it over the chicken and sprinkle with chopped herbs.

Serve with saffron rice and a green salad, or French beans.

Saffron rice

8 oz long grain rice
pinch of saffron (soaked in 1 egg-
  cup of boiling water)
4 rashers of streaky bacon
1 oz butter
1 small onion (finely sliced)
salt and pepper

Method
Cook the rice in plenty of boiling, salted water for about 12 minutes or until tender. Turn into a colander and rinse with a jug of hot water. Leave to drain thoroughly.

Meanwhile, remove rind from bacon. Melt butter in a saucepan, add bacon and fry until brown and crisp. Lift from the pan with a draining spoon and, when cool, crush into small pieces. Add finely-sliced onion to the pan and cook slowly until golden-brown ; fork in the rice and saffron. Toss over heat, adding extra butter if necessary. Season and stir in bacon.

Green salad

Green salads can be of plain lettuce — cabbage, cos, Webb's or Iceberg — depending on the season, or be a mixture of salad greens, such as watercress, sliced cucumber and spring onions. Chicory can also be added in season, but tomato and beetroot (which normally go into an English salad) are best served separately.

Preparation of the salad greens is of great importance. Lettuce leaves should be carefully detached and the outside coarse ones discarded. A fruit or stainless steel knife (not a carbon knife) may be used to trim the bottom stalk, or to quarter the hearts if using them for garnish. If the leaves are too large, pull rather than cut them apart. Wash them well, then swing dry in a salad basket or clean muslin cloth. Make sure this is thoroughly done. If lettuce is at all limp, put it into the refrigerator (in the salad drawer or hydrator) until crisp.

Watercress should be well rinsed in the bunch under the cold tap, then shaken to get rid of the moisture. Carefully pick over and remove some of the stalk, but if this is clean (ie. free from any little hairs) do not discard. These stalks can be snipped into little pieces with scissors and used with chopped herbs, or scattered over vegetable soups, or for a savoury butter. They have a pleasant, slightly peppery taste.

Garlic may be used to flavour, but use it cautiously in a green salad. Either rub the bowl with a peeled clove, or better still, rub a clove well over a crust of French or ordinary bread. Having put the salad into the bowl, bury this 'chapon', as it is called, among the leaves (not forgetting to remove it before serving the salad at the table).

A green salad should be dressed at the last moment, otherwise the leaves will wilt and be unappetising. For a large amount of salad, you will find it easier to mix with its dressing in a really big bowl, and then to transfer it to your salad bowl.

There is, however, a way of dressing the salad where the leaves remain crisp for slightly longer. Sprinkle in enough oil on its own, tossing the leaves all the time to make them glisten. Mix the vinegar (a third of the quantity of oil used) and seasoning together, and sprinkle over the bowl. For a stronger flavour crush garlic with a little salt and add to this dressing. Stir once or twice before serving the salad, so that the dressing is evenly distributed.

Cold chocolate soufflé

4 oz plain block chocolate (roughly chopped)
good ½ pint milk
3 eggs
2 oz caster sugar
5 tablespoons water, or black coffee
½ oz gelatine
¼ pint double cream

To decorate
¼ pint double cream
1 oz plain block chocolate (grated)

6-inch diameter top (No. 2 size) soufflé dish

Method

Prepare soufflé dish by fastening a band of double thickness greaseproof paper with string round the outside to stand 3 inches above top of dish. The chocolate mixture comes above the level of the dish inside this band so that when paper is removed it has the traditional 'raised' appearance of a hot soufflé.

Put ¼ pint of milk into a large pan with the 4 oz chopped chocolate and dissolve over very gentle heat.

Watchpoint Do not let the milk reach more than blood heat (just warm) until the chocolate has melted, or the texture will not be smooth.

Add remaining milk to the pan and bring to scalding (just under boiling) point.

Separate the egg whites from yolks. Work yolks with sugar until thick and light. Tip the chocolate-flavoured milk on to mixture. Return this chocolate custard mixture to saucepan and stir over gentle heat until mixture thickens and coats the back of a wooden spoon. Do not boil. Strain into a large bowl or metal pan and allow to cool. (The metal will allow mixture

Stand the bowl of chocolate custard on ice to help it set. Egg whites and cream should be folded in quickly

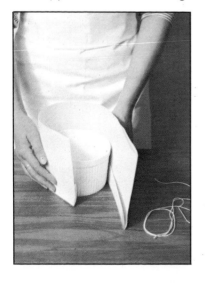

Cold chocolate soufflé continued

to cool more quickly when pan is put on ice to set gelatine.)

Put water or coffee in a saucepan, add gelatine to soak, then dissolve over gentle heat and stir it quickly into the cold custard.

Lightly whip the first $\frac{1}{4}$ pint of cream. Whisk the egg whites until stiff. Stand bowl or pan of custard on ice, stir until just beginning to set (it is important to stir from time to time to thicken mixture evenly). Quickly fold in the cream and egg whites. **Watchpoint** You must fold in the cream and egg whites as soon as mixture begins to set or they will not blend in completely.

Pour into soufflé dish immediately, leave in a cool place to finish setting.

To decorate : whip remaining $\frac{1}{4}$ pint of cream until stiff and spoon on top of soufflé ; pipe rosettes of cream round the edge and sprinkle with grated chocolate.

Before serving remove paper band. It is easy to do this if you first hold the blade of a palette knife in boiling water for a few seconds and then run this between the double thickness of greaseproof paper. The heat loosens the paper and it can be peeled off quite easily.

The finished cold chocolate soufflé. It has the traditional 'raised' appearance of a hot soufflé because the custard mixture is held above the level of the soufflé case by the extra height of the greaseproof paper

Menu 11 Chicken

Starter : Liver pâté

Main course : Cold roast chicken Mojibi, Rice salad

Dessert : Angel cake and strawberries in muscat syrup

Alternative dessert : Austrian coffee cake

TIMETABLE

Order of work

Day before
Roast the chicken.
Blanch and shred pistachio
nuts.
Make the angel cake and
store in an airtight tin.
Make the muscat syrup ;
when cool, store in screw-top
jars.
Make the pâté and keep in
a cool place.

Morning
(Make Austrian coffee cake ;
when cool return it to mould
and soak with coffee mixture.)
Boil the rice, set it aside
after the final draining.
Carve the chicken, dish up
joints and brush with aspic.
Wash lettuce etc. for green
salad.
Make French dressing for
the salads.

Assemble equipment and
ingredients for final cooking
from 6.00 for dinner around
8 pm.

6.00 Whip cream and fill cake.
Slice and macerate straw-
berries in muscat syrup.
Mix rice salad and dish up.
(Turn out Austrian coffee
cake and decorate.)

7.55 Put watercress garnish on
the chicken.
Make toast for pâté and
keep warm.

8.00 Serve first course.
Toss green salad and dish
up just before serving.

Liver pâté

1½ lb pigs, or calves, liver
8 oz very fat bacon (unsmoked),
   or fat from cooked ham
2-3 tablespoons double cream
   (optional)
1 dessertspoon anchovy essence

For béchamel sauce
½ pint milk (infused with slice of
   onion, 6 peppercorns, 1 bayleaf,
   1 blade of mace)
1 oz butter
1 rounded tablespoon plain flour
salt
pepper (ground from mill)
pinch of ground mace, or nutmeg

*1 lb cake tin, or 6-inch diameter top
soufflé dish (No. 2 size)*

Pigs liver is excellent for pâtés, being rich and well flavoured. Calves liver is more expensive but more delicate in flavour.

Method
Remove any ducts and cut liver into small pieces. Take two-thirds of the bacon or ham fat, cut into small pieces and pass all through a mincer and/or work in an electric blender.

To make the béchamel sauce ; put milk and flavourings to infuse. Melt butter in a pan, stir in flour off the heat and gradually blend in strained milk. Stir over heat until boiling, then boil for 2 minutes. Season to taste, add ground mace or nutmeg. Turn into a dish and leave to cool.

Mix the liver with béchamel sauce, cream and anchovy essence. Slice the rest of the bacon or ham fat and use to line the bottom of the shallow tin or soufflé dish.

If liver mixture is not very smooth, pass it through a sieve

or mix in electric blender. Turn into tin or dish, cover with foil, set in a bain-marie half-full of hot water. Bring to boil, then put in oven, pre-set at 350°F or Mark 4, for 45-50 minutes, until firm to the touch. Cover with greaseproof paper, a plate or board and put a light weight (about 2 lb) on top and leave until the next day. Turn out and cut in slices for serving.

Watchpoint If pâté is to be kept for several days, cover top with a little clarified butter and keep in a cool place.

Liver pâté is a good first course , serve it with hot buttered toast

Cold roast Mojibi

Main course

1 roasting chicken (weighing 3-3½ lb)
1½-2 oz butter
sprig of rosemary
salt and pepper
½ pint stock (made from giblets)
1 pint aspic jelly
watercress (to garnish)

Below : turn and baste the chicken during cooking to ensure even browning and a good shape for carving

Method
Set the oven at 400°F or Mark 6.

Rub the chicken well with butter and put a good nut of it inside the bird with the rosemary and seasoning. Place chicken in a roasting tin with half the stock ; cover with a buttered paper and roast for about 1 hour, basting from time to time (a frozen bird will take a little longer). The chicken should be well browned on all sides.

Watchpoint To make sure that your chicken is browned to perfection and keeps a good shape for carving, start cooking with the bird lying on its back. After the first basting, ie. after about 20 minutes cooking time, turn the bird on to its side. When well coloured, turn it on to the other side, baste again and continue cooking, breast side uppermost.

Take up the chicken, tip the remaining stock into the roasting tin and boil up well ; taste for seasoning. Strain liquid through a piece of muslin into a small bowl, leave to cool and when set remove the fat from the top.

When the chicken is quite cold, carve and arrange joints on a serving dish ; cooking juices may be spooned between the joints. Baste with the very cold but still liquid aspic jelly and leave to set. Garnish with bouquets of watercress and serve with rice salad and a green salad (see page 86).

Left : arranging cold cooked chicken joints before coating with aspic jelly

Rice salad

10 oz long grain rice
3 oz pistachio nuts
$\frac{1}{4}$ pint French dressing (see method)
$\frac{1}{4}$ teaspoon ground cinnamon
salt and pepper
3 oz currants

Method

Cook the rice in plenty of salted water for 10-12 minutes, drain and rinse with hot water. Leave rice to drain again, then turn it on to a large flat dish and allow to dry. Blanch, split and shred pistachio nuts.

Prepare the French dressing, using three parts of oil to one part of wine vinegar, and mixing the cinnamon with the salt and pepper.

Mix currants, rice and pistachio nuts together and moisten with the French dressing. Season with extra salt and pepper, if necessary.

Cold roast chicken Mojibi is served with rice salad and a green salad

Angel cake with strawberries in muscat syrup

2 oz plain flour
6½ oz caster sugar
6 egg whites
pinch of salt
¾ teaspoon cream of tartar
3 drops of vanilla essence
2 drops of almond essence

To finish
¾ pint double cream
1 teaspoon caster sugar
2-3 drops of vanilla essence
1 lb strawberries
¼ pint muscat syrup

8-9 inch diameter angel cake tin (with funnelled base)

After layering and covering the cake with cream, pipe rosettes on top

Method
Set the oven at 375°F or Mark 5.

Sift the flour and 3½ oz of the caster sugar three times and set aside.

Place the egg whites, salt and cream of tartar in a large dry pudding basin and whisk with a rotary beater until mixture is foamy. Add remaining 3 oz of sugar, 2 tablespoons at a time, and the essences and continue beating until the mixture will stand in peaks. Carefully fold in the sifted flour and sugar.

Turn the mixture into the clean dry cake tin, level the surface and draw a knife through the mixture to break any air bubbles. Bake the cake in pre-set hot oven for 30-35 minutes or until no imprint remains when you lightly touch the top with your finger.

When the cake is done, turn it upside down on a wire rack and leave until quite cold; it will fall easily from the tin. Cut the cake in three layers with a serrated-edge knife.

Watchpoint A serrated-edge knife is important as the cake's texture is very delicate. Use a sawing movement for best results.

Lightly whip the cream, then add the sugar and vanilla essence and continue whisking until thick. Spread each layer with cream, re-shape cake and cover with the whipped cream. Decorate the top and outside edge of the cake with rosettes of cream and a few whole berries.

Hull the remaining strawberries and cut in thick slices. Spoon muscat syrup over them; serve in a sauce boat or glass bowl.

Muscat syrup

Wash, top and tail 3 lb of goose-berries, put in a pan with $\frac{1}{2}$ pint water and simmer until they are soft. Add $2\frac{3}{4}$ lb lump sugar, dissolve over gentle heat and bring to the boil. Tie 8 large elder-flowers in a piece of muslin and add to the syrup. Draw pan aside and leave to infuse for 7-10 minutes. Strain syrup through muslin. Use as required and sterilise remainder for storing.

Angel cake with strawberries, and extra sliced ones served in muscat syrup

Austrian coffee cake
Alternative dessert

6 oz butter
6 oz caster sugar
3 eggs (beaten)
6 oz self-raising flour
pinch of salt
½ pint strong black coffee
sugar and rum or brandy (to taste)
½ pint double cream (whipped)
1-2 drops of vanilla essence
almonds (browned)

Ring mould (1½ pints capacity) or 8-inch diameter cake tin

Austrian coffee cake is one of the more decorative sweets. The cake is soaked in sweetened coffee that has been flavoured with rum or brandy, it is then covered with whipped cream and browned almonds

Method
Set the oven at 375°F or Mark 5. Cream the butter in a bowl, add the sugar and cream again until light and fluffy. Beat in the eggs a little at a time and lastly fold in the sifted flour and salt with a metal spoon. Turn the mixture into the greased ring mould and bake for about 25 minutes, or 35-40 minutes if using a cake tin.

When cooked, take cake out of oven, turn out and set aside to cool. When cold, return to mould. Sweeten the coffee to taste, and flavour with rum or brandy. Pour slowly over cake while still in mould. Turn out for serving and coat with the cream, sweetened and flavoured with vanilla essence. Decorate with the browned almonds.

Menu 12 Chicken

Serves 4

Starter : Coquilles St. Jacques Dugléré

Main course : Spring chicken alsacienne, new potatoes, green beans

Dessert : Raspberry parfait

Alternative starter : Mussel chowder

TIMETABLE

Day before
Make raspberries into a purée, put in refrigerator or icebox.
Split poussins and make stock.

Morning
Prepare vegetable accompaniments to chicken dish, but do not slice the potatoes yet — leave in cold water.
Cook scallops and potatoes and dish up in shells for reheating.
(Prepare vegetables and parsley for chowder.)

Assemble equipment for final cooking from 6.00 for dinner around 8 pm.

Order of work

6.00 (Prepare chowder, leave in saucepan for reheating.)
Whip cream for parfait, cover and put in refrigerator.

6.50 Start chicken.
Cook beans, drain and refresh.
Slice potatoes, put on top of stove to cook.
If preparing parfait in advance, do so now.
Put scallops on shelf under chicken to heat.

7.30 Put chicken in moderate oven to keep warm, and potatoes to continue cooking.
Make sauce for chicken and keep warm in a double saucepan / bain-marie.
Toss beans in butter, dish up and keep warm.

7.45 (Put chowder over gentle heat to warm.)
If parfait is to be put together between courses, take raspberry purée from ice compartment and put beside whipped cream in refrigerator.
(Add parsley to chowder and serve.) Dish potatoes.
Spoon sauce over chicken just before taking to table.
Whip egg whites and put parfait together between courses.

8.00 Serve first course.

Coquilles St. Jacques Dugléré

6-8 scallops (fresh or frozen)
1 shallot, or small onion (sliced)
salt
6 peppercorns
$\frac{1}{2}$ bayleaf
scant $\frac{1}{4}$ pint water
squeeze of lemon juice
2 tomatoes
1 oz butter
1 rounded tablespoon plain flour
$\frac{1}{4}$ pint creamy milk
1 teaspoon finely chopped parsley
browned breadcrumbs
little extra butter

For potato purée
1 lb potatoes
$\frac{1}{2}$ oz butter
1 tablespoon hot milk

4 scallop shells

Method

First make the potato purée. Peel and boil potatoes, drain and dry them, then beat to a purée (or put through a sieve) with butter and milk.

Wash the scallops and put in a pan with the sliced shallot or onion, seasonings and bayleaf. Pour on the water, add the lemon juice and poach gently for 5 minutes.

Watchpoint Do not let the scallops boil because this toughens them.

Scald and skin the tomatoes, cut in four, remove seeds, then cut flesh in four again.

Melt the butter in a pan, remove from heat and stir in the flour. Blend in the liquid strained from the scallops. Stir over gentle heat until liquid starts to thicken, then add the milk and bring to the boil. Simmer for 2-3 minutes, taste for seasoning, then add prepared tomatoes and chopped parsley.

Slice or quarter the scallops and put into 4-6 buttered, deep scallop shells ; spoon over the sauce. Pipe potato purée round each shell, sprinkle lightly with browned breadcrumbs and a few tiny shavings of the extra butter.

If you prepare this dish early in the day, put it in a hot oven (about 400°F or Mark 6) for 10-15 minutes to heat through. If it is freshly cooked and scallops, potato and sauce are hot, put under the grill to brown the potatoes.

How to prepare scallops

Scallops, when alive, have their shells tightly closed, but they are usually bought ready prepared (opened and cleaned).

The easiest way to open them yourself is to put the shells into a hot oven for 4-5 minutes. The heat will cause the shells to gape. Carefully scrape away the fringe or beard which surrounds the scallop, attached to the flat shell, and the black thread (the intestine) which lies round it.

Then slip a sharp knife under the scallop to detach it and the roe from the shell. Scrub the shells thoroughly, and use for serving.

Frozen scallops are already prepared.

Top : Spooning sauce over the cooked scallops before piping round with potato.
Above : Finished scallops, with border of potato purée after browning under the grill

Spring chicken alsacienne

3 double poussins (baby chickens,
 6-10 weeks old)
1 tablespoon oil
1 oz butter
salt and pepper
1½ wineglasses Alsatian white wine
1 teaspoon arrowroot
¼ pint strong chicken stock (made
 from the giblets and bones)
1 small can pâté de foie (2½ oz)
3 tablespoons double cream
bunch of watercress (to garnish)

This quantity of poussins allows
for some second helpings.

Method
Split the poussins in two and
cut away the backbone and rib-
cage ; put these to cook in a pan,
with the giblets and water to
cover, to make stock.

Heat the oil in sauté pan or
shallow casserole, add the butter
and as it foams put in the birds,
skin side down. Season, and
cook slowly for 15-20 minutes
until golden-brown. Turn the
birds and moisten with half the
wine, cover and continue
cooking very gently until tender
(about 20-30 minutes). Dish up
the chicken and keep hot.

Tip the remaining wine into
the pan, bring to the boil, scrape
the bottom and sides of the pan
well and allow to reduce to half
the quantity. Mix the arrowroot
with half the stock and set aside.

1 *Cutting the backbone from the split
poussin*
2 *Cutting rib-cage after removing
backbone*

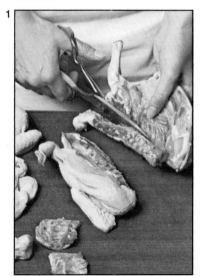

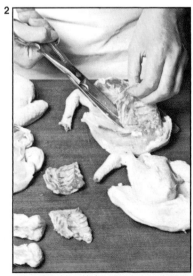

Rub the pâté de foie through a nylon strainer, then mix it with the remaining stock. Thicken the juices in the pan with the arrowroot, bring to the boil and strain into a small pan. Add the pâté mixture and cream. Reheat carefully, taste for seasoning and then spoon sauce over the chicken.

Serve with new potatoes and sliced green beans.

Spring chicken alsacienne, served with the sauce spooned over it and garnished with watercress. New potatoes and green beans accompany it

Raspberry parfait

1 lb frozen raspberries (preferably
without sugar), or fresh, if
available
2 egg whites
4 oz caster sugar
$\frac{1}{2}$ pint double cream

Method

Rub the raspberries through a
nylon strainer, put resulting
purée in refrigerator ice trays
and leave in freezing compartment overnight. If you have a
home freezer or a good size ice
box, the purée can be put in a
polythene container.

About 1 hour before serving,
whisk the egg whites until stiff
with an electric or rotary beater,
then add the sugar, 1 tablespoon
at a time, and continue beating
until the mixture stands in peaks.
Whisk the cream lightly until a
little lifted on the whisk and
allowed to fall leaves a trail.

Remove the ice trays from
the refrigerator and work the
raspberry purée with a wooden
spoon to break down the ice
crystals, or if purée is in a deep
container you can beat it with
a whisk.

Fold the cream and egg whites
together and then quickly but
carefully fold in the semi-frozen
raspberry purée. Pile into tall
glasses or a crystal bowl and
keep in the coolest part of the
refrigerator until wanted.

Watchpoint This parfait is really
at its very best if put together
between courses. With everything
to hand — a chilled bowl or
glasses and ready-whipped
cream waiting in the refrigerator
— you could do it in about 8
minutes. You might feel a little
breathless after beating the egg
whites and sugar but you will
have the satisfaction of knowing

your parfait is being served
when it is at the point of perfection.

1 *Consistency of whisked egg
whites and sugar mixture before
it is combined with the whipped
cream*
2 *Raspberry purée being blended
with the egg white and cream
mixture*

Dessert

Mussel chowder

1 can mussels (14 oz)
4 oz green streaky bacon
  (unsmoked)
1 large onion (chopped)
1 stick of celery (chopped)
1 green pepper (blanched and
  chopped)
2 medium-size potatoes (diced)
1 small bayleaf
$\frac{3}{4}$ pint water
salt and pepper
$1\frac{1}{4}$ oz plain flour
1 pint milk
1 dessertspoon chopped parsley

Chowder, an American speciality, is a soup stew made from shellfish (or white fish) with vegetables and unsmoked bacon or salt pork, according to the recipe.

Method

Remove the rind and cut bacon into dice ; sizzle gently in a dry pan until turning colour, then add the onion and celery and cook until golden-brown. Add the green pepper, potatoes, bayleaf and water and bring to the boil. Season, and simmer until potatoes are tender, then draw pan aside.

Blend the flour with $\frac{1}{2}$ cup of the milk and add to the chowder ; stir until boiling. Heat the rest of the milk and add to the chowder with the drained mussels ; simmer 4-5 minutes before turning into a soup tureen, Scatter parsley over top.

Menu 13 Duck

Starter : Couronne of shrimps in aspic

Main course : Sauté of duck with Burgundy, Sicilian
potatoes, brussels sprouts

Dessert : Pears 'en douillon'

Alternative starter : Courgettes maison

TIMETABLE

Order of work

Day before
Prepare the stock for
couronne of shrimps.
Make rough puff pastry for
pears and keep in
refrigerator.

Morning
Brown the ducks and allow
to cool ; cut into pieces,
cover and leave until
evening.
Prepare Sicilian potatoes
and leave on a buttered
baking sheet ready for
browning.
Clarify the aspic jelly for
couronne of shrimps ; cut
the garnish of tomato and
celery.
Make the mayonnaise.
Prepare and bake the pears.
Finish the couronne of
shrimps, set aside in a cool
place.
(Blanch courgettes and
prepare them ready for
reheating with mornay sauce.)

Assemble ingredients and
equipment for final cooking
from 6.30 for dinner around
8 pm.

6.30 Set oven at 400°F or
Mark 6.
Dish up couronne of
shrimps and cut brown
bread and butter to
accompany.
Add tomato juice to
mayonnaise.

7.00 Put potatoes in oven to
brown, then dish up
and keep warm. Turn
oven down to lowest
setting.
(Turn oven up for
courgettes.)

7.15 Sauté and complete the
duck, dish up and keep
warm. Cook the brussels
sprouts or chosen green
vegetable.
(Make mornay sauce for
courgettes.)

7.45 (Put courgettes to bake.
Turn down oven when
finished.)

8.00 Put pears in bottom of
oven to heat.
Serve first course.

Couronne of shrimps in aspic

6 oz shrimps, or prawns (shelled)
4 tomatoes
1 head of celery, or 1 bunch of
   watercress
¼ pint mayonnaise

For aspic jelly
1½ pints well-seasoned fish, or
   light chicken, stock
1½ oz gelatine
2 egg whites
¼ pint white wine
squeeze of lemon juice

*Ring, or border, mould (1½-1¾ pints
   capacity)*

1 *Arranging the tomato quarters,
rounded sides down with points
facing outwards, on a layer of cool
aspic*
2 *Placing some shrimps on the
tomatoes, before layering the remainder alternately with aspic*

Method
First prepare aspic jelly : put
the stock and gelatine into a
scalded pan and dissolve it
over gentle heat. Whip the egg
whites to a froth and add them
to the pan with the wine and
lemon juice ; whisk over steady
heat until boiling point is
reached, then allow liquid to
boil to the top of the pan undisturbed. Draw pan aside without
breaking the crust on top and
leave jelly to settle. Then boil
it up twice more in the same
way, leave it to stand for 5 minutes, pour it through a scalded
cloth and reserve.

Scald and skin the tomatoes,
cut them in four, scoop out the
seeds into a small strainer and
reserve the juice. Line the mould
with a little cool aspic, arrange
the quarters of tomato on this,
rounded side down, and with the
points towards the outer rim of
the mould. Spoon over enough
cold but still liquid aspic to hold
the tomatoes in position and
leave to set. Fill the mould
alternately with shrimps (or
prawns) and cool aspic, and
leave to set.

1

2

Cut the celery into 2-inch lengths, then shred them into julienne strips. Leave these to soak and curl up in ice-cold water for about 30 minutes, then drain thoroughly.

To turn out the mould dip it into warm water, put your serving plate or dish over it, quickly turn it over; the jelly should slide out easily. Fill the centre with the celery curls (or washed sprigs of watercress). Mix the mayonnaise with the juice strained from the tomato seeds and serve this separately. Accompany with brown bread and butter.

Sauté of duck with Burgundy

2 medium-size ducks, or ducklings
1 tablespoon oil or $\frac{1}{2}$ oz butter
1 medium-size onion (finely sliced)
scant 1 oz butter (optional)
6-8 oz button mushrooms
2 wineglasses red Burgundy
   (preferably Mâcon)
1 wineglass jellied stock
salt and pepper
kneaded butter
fried croûtes of bread (to garnish)
   — optional

This recipe is also good to use for wild duck.

Method
Quickly brown the ducks all over in the oil (or the $\frac{1}{2}$ oz butter) in a large pan (they may have to be done one at a time).
Note : the reason for browning the ducks is to extract some of the fat, as otherwise the sauce would be too greasy. Butter can be used in place of the oil, if preferred from the point of view of flavour.

Remove birds from the pan and leave to cool a little. Then divide them into four, first cutting down through the breastbone with scissors and then on either side of the backbone through the rib cage ; cut each half into two just above the leg, and set aside. (The backbones can then be used for stock for a stew.) Add the onion to the pan, in which there should be about 1-2 tablespoons of the duck fat (if preferred, use the scant oz of butter). Allow the onion to brown slightly, then add the mushrooms, whole or sliced according to size, and sauté briskly for 2-3 minutes.

Heat the wine in a small pan, reduce it and then add to the pan with the stock. Stir until it boils, season, put in the pieces of duck, cover and simmer for 10 minutes. The duckling, or wild duck, should be kept slightly pink, but for older birds continue to cook until tender (35-40 minutes).

When ready to serve, trim the joints with scissors, if necessary, to remove any ugly bones. Pile meat up in a serving dish, thicken the sauce slightly with kneaded butter, reboil and spoon over the dish.
Note : as with most sautés, there should be just enough sauce to coat the dish nicely and to allow about 2 tablespoons extra for each guest.

This dish may be garnished with fried croûtes of bread. Serve with Sicilian potatoes and brussels sprouts (if possible, the small 'red' home-grown variety).

Sicilian potatoes

$\frac{1}{2}$-$\frac{3}{4}$ lb potatoes (3-4 medium-size ones)
1 small orange (preferably a blood orange)
pinch of bicarbonate of soda
4 oz butter
2 shallots (finely chopped)
salt and pepper
1 egg yolk (optional)

Method
First put the orange in a pan of water with a pinch of bicarbonate of soda and boil for 45-50 minutes. Peel the potatoes, then boil, drain and dry well and crush with a potato masher or push through a sieve. Turn them into a basin.

Meanwhile set the oven at 400°F or Mark 6. Drain the

orange, cut in four and remove any pips, then finely chop the quarters (including peel). Melt 2 oz of the butter in a small saucepan, add the shallot and cook until coloured ; cook for 1-2 minutes more, then add the chopped orange. Cook onion mixture, without the lid, until turning colour. Then turn into the sieved potato ; mix with a fork, season well, add 1 oz butter and the egg yolk, if wished.

Melt the remainder of the butter, brush two baking sheets with it, then shape the mixture into large 'marbles'. Put these down the baking sheet at intervals and, with the prongs of a fork, flatten each marble to about $\frac{1}{4}$ inch thick. Bake in the pre-set hot oven for about 10-15 minutes or until well browned. Take the baking sheets out of the oven, slip a palette knife under each potato 'cake' and serve them overlapping on a hot dish, with the underside uppermost.

Note : the underside of the potatoes should be brown and practically caramelised so that these cakes are almost crisp to eat. They also make good cocktail savouries.

Pears 'en douillon'

4-6 ripe dessert pears
12 oz quantity of rough puff
  pastry (chilled)
2 tablespoons granulated sugar
2 tablespoons brandy
1 egg (beaten)
6 tablespoons redcurrant jelly
1-inch piece of angelica (cut in
  strips)
whipped cream (to serve)

1 *Keep pears upright when wrapping
in pastry to prevent brandy running
out*
2 *Decorating pears with stars, cut
from pastry trimmings, before baking*

Method

Roll out pastry fairly thinly and cut into squares, each large enough to enclose one pear. Set the oven at 425°F or Mark 7.

Peel the pears, remove the stalk and hollow the centre to remove the core very carefully ; do not cut right through the pear. Fill the hole with sugar and brandy. Turn each square of pastry over, then, keeping pear upright, shape pastry around each one, leaving a hole at the top. Brush them with beaten egg, decorate with a few stars or fancy shapes cut from pastry trimmings and brush again with egg. Bake upright in the pre-set hot oven for about 15-20 minutes until the pastry is golden-brown and crisp.

Meanwhile beat the redcurrant jelly until smooth and runny, rub through a strainer into a small pan and heat gently. Pour a little warm redcurrant jelly into each pear and put a piece of angelica in the top to resemble a stalk. Serve with a bowl of whipped cream.

A pear 'en douillon', decorated with angelica and served with cream

Courgettes maison

8 small courgettes
4 tomatoes
1 oz butter
1 shallot (finely chopped)
1 teaspoon paprika pepper
salt and pepper
½ lb shelled prawns
1 tablespoon grated Parmesan cheese (for dusting)

For mornay sauce
1 oz butter
1 oz plain flour
½ pint milk
2 oz Parmesan cheese (grated)

1 *Carefully scooping out the flesh of the cooked courgettes with a teaspoon*
2 *Filling courgette cases with the prawn and tomato mixture before spooning over mornay sauce and browning in oven*

Method
Trim each end of the courgettes, cook whole for 5 minutes in boiling salted water, then drain and refresh them. Remove a thin slice lengthways from each courgette, carefully scoop out the flesh with the point of a teaspoon and chop it. Scald and skin the tomatoes ; cut in four, discard the seeds and chop flesh coarsely.

Melt the butter in a saucepan, add the chopped shallot and cook, covered, until quite soft but not brown ; add the paprika, chopped courgette flesh and tomatoes. Season and cook briskly for 2-3 minutes. Stir in the prawns.

Put the courgette cases in a buttered gratin dish and fill them with the tomato and prawn mixture. Prepare mornay sauce and spoon it over the courgettes ; dust with cheese. Brown in oven at 425°F or Mark 7 for 10-12 minutes.

Menu 14 Ham

Starter : French onion soup

Main course : Ham Véronique

Dessert : Brown bread cream with damson sauce

Alternative main course : Escalopes of veal with lemon

TIMETABLE

Order of work

Morning
Make soup.
Prepare vegetables.
Make brown bread cream
and damson sauce.
Prepare grapes, add lemon
juice and keep covered in
a bowl.
(Prepare the stuffing for veal,
beat escalopes and roll up
paupiettes.)

Assemble ingredients and
equipment for final cooking
from 6.00 for dinner around
8 pm.

6.00 Put ham on to cook.
Dish up brown bread
cream and sauce.

7.00 (Start cooking veal.)

7.15 Cook vegetables.

7.30 Make sauce for ham.
(Dish up paupiettes and
keep warm ; reduce gravy.)

7.40 Reheat soup. Toss vegetables in butter to reheat
and dish up. Dish up ham
and keep warm.

8.00 Serve first course, adding
garnish to soup just
before serving.

French onion soup

3 onions
1 oz butter
1½ pints good stock
salt and pepper
glass Champagne (optional)
1½ oz each of Gruyère and
    Parmesan cheese (grated)
1 slice of French bread per
    person
1 egg per person (for serving)

For this soup a really good
beef stock is needed. If a little
meat can be added to the stock
bones, so much the better.

Method
Have ready small earthenware
soup pots with lids (marmites).
Slice or chop the onions finely
and colour them to a golden-
brown in butter in a frying pan.
Bring the stock to the boil
and add the onions ; season,
simmer for 5 minutes, then add
the Champagne, if using it.

Mix the cheeses together and
sprinkle a little on the slices of
bread ; put a slice into each
marmite, then pour on the
boiling soup. Put on the lids
and serve. Alongside each place
have a small dish of the remaining cheese and a fresh egg.
Each guest breaks the raw egg
into the soup, adds the cheese
and beats it up with a fork. The
soup must be really boiling so
that the egg cooks a little and
thickens the broth slightly.

Ham Véronique

1 corner gammon, or cut of
   middle gammon
few root vegetables (sliced) —
   for flavouring
bouquet garni
$\frac{1}{2}$ lb green grapes
lemon juice

For sauce
1 wineglass dry white wine
1 dessertspoon finely chopped
   onion
2 egg yolks
3 oz butter

For roux
1 oz butter
1 rounded tablespoon plain flour
$\frac{1}{2}$-$\frac{3}{4}$ pint veal stock
$\frac{1}{8}$ pint single cream, or top of milk

*When cooked ham has cooled a little,
the skin should be peeled off carefully*

Method

Cover the gammon with water
and simmer with the sliced
vegetables and bouquet garni,
allowing 20 minutes per lb and
20 minutes over. Cool a little in
the liquid.

Peel and pip the grapes, add
a few drops of lemon juice and
keep covered in a bowl.

To prepare sauce : boil the
wine with the onion to reduce
by about a third. Cream egg
yolks well, then strain on the
wine, add about $\frac{1}{2}$ oz of the
butter and work the mixture in a
bain-marie (or double saucepan) until thick. Then add the
rest of the butter, a little at a
time, until the sauce has the
consistency of thick cream, but
do not boil. Set aside.

To prepare the roux : melt
1 oz butter in a pan, add flour,
cook for 1 minute, then pour
on the stock. Blend and stir
until boiling. Cook for a few
minutes. Draw pan aside, beat
in butter sauce, add cream or
milk and reheat slowly. Do not
allow to boil. Add the grapes
and set aside.

Take up the ham, remove
skin, slice and arrange in a dish.
Coat with a little of the sauce
and serve the rest separately.
Serve with new potatoes and a
green vegetable of your choice.

Raw ingredients for flavouring ham Véronique

Brown bread cream with damson sauce

3 slices wholemeal bread (2-3
days old)
1 tablespoon caster sugar
$\frac{3}{4}$ pint milk
pared rind and juice of $\frac{1}{2}$ lemon
3 egg yolks
1$\frac{1}{2}$ oz caster sugar
5 tablespoons water
$\frac{1}{2}$ oz gelatine
$\frac{1}{4}$ pint double cream
$\frac{1}{2}$ lb damsons
$\frac{1}{2}$ pint water
4 tablespoons granulated sugar

*Decorative mould, or glass bowl
(1$\frac{1}{4}$-1$\frac{1}{2}$ pints capacity)*

Method

Remove the crusts from the
bread and rub through a wire
sieve or reduce to crumbs a
little at a time in a liquidiser.
Set the oven at 350°F or Mark 4.
Spread out the crumbs on a
sheet of greaseproof paper on a
baking sheet, dust with the tablespoon of caster sugar and put
in the pre-set moderate oven to
brown. Allow to cool.

Watchpoint Great care must be
taken to brown the crumbs as
evenly as possible, so turn them
with a fork several times while
they are browning. The time the
crumbs take to brown will
depend on the freshness of the
bread, but allow 10 minutes —
they must be very crisp.

Heat the milk with the lemon
rind to scalding point, cover and
leave to infuse. Lightly oil the
mould, or have ready the glass
bowl. Work the egg yolks and
1$\frac{1}{2}$ oz caster sugar together with
a wooden spoon until thick and
light in colour, strain on the hot
milk. Pour the water and lemon
juice on to the gelatine and
leave soaking. Return the egg
and milk mixture to the rinsed
saucepan and stir briskly over
heat until it thickens and coats
the back of the wooden spoon.
Strain quickly into a large bowl,
add the soaked gelatine, stir
until dissolved and then leave
to cool, but not in a refrigerator.

When the custard is quite
cold, tip it into a thin saucepan.
Lightly whip the cream and fold
it into the custard. Stand the
saucepan in a bowl of cold water
with a few ice cubes added. Stir
gently until the custard is on the
point of setting, then quickly
fold in the crisp brown breadcrumbs. Pour it into the prepared
mould or glass bowl, cover and
leave in the refrigerator, or in a
cool place, for 1-2 hours to set.

Cook the damsons with the
water and granulated sugar
until soft and pulpy, then rub
through a strainer. (Damson jelly
can also be used ; just melt it in
a saucepan over heat with 2-3
tablespoons of water, then cool.)
To serve, turn the cream out of
the mould and pour the sauce
over or around it. Or, if the
cream is served from the glass
bowl, decorate with a little extra
cream and hand the sauce
separately.

1 *Crumbs made from stale wholemeal bread are dusted with sugar
before being browned in the oven*
2 *When the chilled custard, with
cream added, is on the point of
setting, the breadcrumbs are folded
into it*

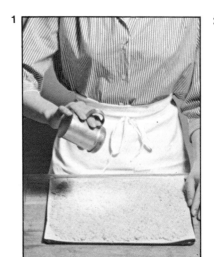

Escalopes of veal with lemon

4-6 veal escalopes
butter
1 onion (chopped)
1 wineglass white wine
pared rind of $\frac{1}{2}$ lemon
1 wineglass stock
kneaded butter

For stuffing
1 medium-size onion (finely chopped)
1 oz butter
6 oz cooked ham (finely chopped, or minced)
3 tablespoons fresh white breadcrumbs
1 tablespoon mixed chopped herbs (lemon thyme and parsley)
1 small egg (beaten)

Method
Beat the escalopes out as thin as possible. Then prepare the stuffing. Soften the onion in the butter, then add to the ham with the crumbs, herbs and beaten egg. Spread this on the escalopes, roll them up and tie.

Brown the escalopes carefully in butter, add the onion and, after a few minutes, the wine, lemon rind and stock. Cover and simmer gently for 20-25 minutes.

Take up the paupiettes, remove the strings and dish up on a bed of creamed potatoes. Reduce the gravy well and thicken it very slightly with a little kneaded butter. Strain over the dish. Garnish with small, whole carrots.

Menu 15 Veal

Starter : Iced cucumber soup

Main course : Roast stuffed veal, Petits pois à la française, Fondant potatoes

Dessert : Tipsy cake

Alternative starter : Crab mousse

TIMETABLE

Order of work

Day before
Make soup (or crab mousse) and store in refrigerator. Stuff veal, spread with butter and wrap in foil ready for cooking. Make sponge for tipsy cake. Make sugar syrup for tipsy cake. Wash and shred lettuce, shell peas and prepare spring onions. Keep in polythene bag in refrigerator ready for cooking next day.

Morning
Assemble ingredients and equipment for final cooking from 5.30 for dinner at 8 pm.

5.30 Set oven.

6.00 Put meat to cook.
Put meat to cook.
Soak, fill and dish up tipsy cake.
(Prepare cucumber salad to accompany crab mousse, and butter bread.)

6.50 Turn meat.

7.25 Start cooking the potatoes and peas.

7.40 Take up meat, keep in foil and turn gas oven to lowest setting or turn off electric oven.
Make gravy.
Dish up vegetables and meat.
Add cream and mint to soup.

8.00 Serve first course.

Iced cucumber soup

2 medium-size cucumber
2 shallots, or 1 medium-size onion
    (finely chopped)
3 pints chicken stock
2 oz butter
2 tablespoons plain flour
salt and pepper
3 egg yolks
6-8 tablespoons double cream
2-3 drops of green edible colouring

To garnish
1 tablespoon finely chopped mint,
    or chives
3 tablespoons double cream (very
    lightly whipped)

Method

Peel cucumbers and cut into $\frac{1}{2}$ inch slices ; simmer in a pan with shallot and stock for 15-20 minutes until soft. Rub through a nylon strainer or work in a liquidiser until smooth. Melt the butter, add the flour and cook until straw-coloured and marbled in appearance. Blend in the cucumber liquid, stir until boiling, then season and simmer for 2-3 minutes.

Work the yolks and cream together in a bowl with a wooden spoon, draw the soup off the heat and then very slowly add about 3-4 tablespoons of the hot soup to this liaison. Return this to the saucepan a little at a time, then reheat gently without boiling until the soup has thickened. Colour the soup very delicately, adjust seasoning, and pour into a container ready for chilling. Cover soup to prevent a skin forming and when cold place it in refrigerator or in a bowl packed with ice to chill.

Remember to chill the tureen and soup cups before serving. Put a rounded teaspoon of cream in each cup, or the equivalent in a tureen, and stir it in gently to give the soup a streaky look ; sprinkle with mint or chives. If the day is chilly, serve the soup hot.

Adding hot soup to liaison of egg yolks and cream before blending it in

Roast stuffed veal

4 lb fillet, or boned shoulder, of veal
2 oz butter

For stuffing
1 cup (3 oz) fresh white breadcrumbs
1 tablespoon chopped parsley
1 teaspoon mixed dried herbs
grated rind of ½ lemon
salt and pepper
1 medium-size onion (finely chopped)
2 oz butter
juice of ½ lemon
a little beaten egg

For gravy
1 tablespoon plain flour
¾ pint veal, or chicken, stock

Veal is a very good-tempered meat and will keep hot well. To cut down work to the minimum we suggest roasting it in foil ; this will help keep the meat moist and cut out the necessity for basting, as well as preventing the oven from getting splashed.

Method
Set oven at 400°F or Mark 6. First prepare the stuffing : place the crumbs, herbs, lemon rind and seasoning in a basin. Put the onion in a pan, cover with cold water, bring to the boil and cook for 5 minutes. Drain and return to the pan with the butter ; cover with greaseproof paper, pressed well down on onion, and lid and cook gently for 7-8 minutes.

Stir the softened onion into the crumbs and mix with the lemon juice and just enough beaten egg to bind. Stuff the meat, roll up and secure with poultry pins or sew with trussing needle and fine string. Spread joint with butter and wrap in foil. Set in a roasting tin and cook in the pre-set oven for 1 hour and 40 minutes (25 minutes per lb) ; turn the meat after 50 minutes and at the end of the cooking time open up the foil ; baste the meat well with the juices and continue for a further 20-25 minutes until nicely brown on all sides.

Take up the meat, place on the serving dish and keep warm while preparing the gravy. Cook the juices left in the roasting tin over gentle heat until brown and sticky, blend in the flour and stock and stir until boiling ; simmer for 3-5 minutes, adjust the seasoning and strain into a sauce boat. Serve with new potatoes and petits pois à la française.

Petits pois à la française

4 lb young green peas (2 pints shelled)
1 Cos lettuce (shredded)
12-24 small spring onions (cut in 2-inch lengths)
1 dessertspoon granulated sugar
bouquet garni
2 oz butter
¼ pint cold water
salt

Method
Put the peas in a pan with the shredded lettuce, spring onions, sugar, herbs and half the butter ; add the water. Instead of a lid, cover the pan with a deep plate filled with cold water and cook quickly for 25 minutes.
Note : the purpose of this plate

containing cold water is to condense the steam as it rises from the peas while they cook. As the water in the plate evaporates, add more cold water.

Just 2 minutes before serving remove the bouquet garni, then add the remaining butter and salt to taste and shake the pan well to mix. Turn peas into a hot vegetable dish for serving.

Tipsy cake

2¼ oz plain flour
2½ oz fécule (potato flour), or
   arrowroot
pinch of salt
5 eggs
10 oz caster sugar
grated rind of 1 lemon

For soaking the cake
sugar syrup (made with 4 oz
   granulated sugar and 6 tablespoons water)
3 wineglasses sweet white wine
2 tablespoons brandy

To finish
1 lb fresh raspberries
½ pint double cream
¼ pint single cream
1 teaspoon vanilla-flavoured sugar

8½-9 inch diameter cake tin

Method
Grease and flour cake tin and set oven at 350°F or Mark 4. Sift the flours together with a pinch of salt. Put 3 whole eggs, 2 yolks and sugar into a mixing bowl and whisk over hot water until thick and mousse-like (or at a high speed on an electric mixer, without heat). Whisk the 2 egg whites until stiff and, using a metal spoon, fold into the mixture with the sifted flours and grated lemon rind. Turn into the prepared cake tin and bake for about 45-60 minutes. When cake is cool, cut round and down into the centre of the cake top, using a serrated-edge knife to remove a 'cone-shaped' piece about 2½ inches deep and approximately 5-6 inches wide at the top.

Add the wine and brandy to the sugar syrup. Whip the double cream until it begins to thicken, then add the single cream gradually, whisking all the time ; when thick, fold in the sugar. Soak the cake with two-thirds of the sweetened wine and fill with half the cream and raspberries. Replace the 'cone' and moisten the cake again with wine. Spoon over the remaining cream and decorate with the raspberries.

Cutting cooled cake with serrated knife to remove cone-shaped piece

Finished tipsy cake topped with whipped cream and decorated with whole raspberries

Crab mousse

1 lb crab meat ($\frac{1}{2}$ white, $\frac{1}{2}$ dark)
$\frac{1}{2}$ pint velouté sauce
$\frac{1}{2}$ oz gelatine
$2\frac{1}{2}$ fl oz white wine
$\frac{1}{2}$ pint mayonnaise
$\frac{1}{4}$ pint double cream (lightly
  whipped)

For garnish
1 cucumber
4 tablespoons French dressing
$\frac{1}{2}$ teaspoon paprika pepper
Tabasco sauce

*7-inch diameter top (No. 1 size)
  soufflé dish, or cake tin*

Method
Oil the dish or tin. Prepare the velouté sauce, work in the dark crab meat and leave to cool. Soak the gelatine in wine, dissolve it over heat and then stir it into velouté sauce with the mayonnaise. Fold the flaked white crab meat into the mixture with the cream. Turn mousse into the prepared dish or tin and leave it to set.

Meanwhile, slice the cucumber, sprinkle it with salt and leave pressed between two plates for 30 minutes, then drain. Flavour the French dressing with paprika and a good dash of Tabasco and mix with cucumber. Turn mousse on to a serving dish and spoon cucumber over it.

Velouté sauce

1 oz butter
1 oz flour
$\frac{1}{2}$ pint chicken stock
$2\frac{1}{2}$ fl oz top of milk
salt and pepper
squeeze of lemon juice

For liaison (optional)
1 egg yolk (lightly beaten)
2 tablespoons cream

Method
Melt butter in a saucepan, stir in flour and cook for about 5 seconds. When roux is colour of pale straw, draw pan aside and cool slightly before pouring on stock.

Blend, return to heat and stir until thick. Add top of milk, season and bring to boil. Cook 4-5 minutes when sauce should be a syrupy consistency. If using a liaison, prepare by mixing egg yolk and cream together and then stir into sauce. Add lemon juice. Remove pan from heat.
Watchpoint Be careful not to let sauce boil after liaison has been added, otherwise the mixture will curdle.

Menu 16 Fish

Starter : Cream of beetroot soup

Main course : Turbot with lobster sauce

Dessert : Pineapple upside - down cake

Alternative dessert : Almond and raspberry flan

TIMETABLE

Order of work

Day before
Make soup and sieve, but
do not add cornflour and
cream thickening.
Make court bouillon for fish.
Peel and slice the pineapple
and cook in the syrup.

Morning
Prepare potatoes.
Prepare tin for cake,
arranging fruit in position.
Make the flan but do not
add the cream.
Assemble ingredients and
equipment for final cooking
from 6.00 or dinner at 8 pm.

6.00 Set oven and make cake.

6.15 Put cake in oven.
Whip cream or make hard
sauce.

6.50 Put on fish.
(Whip cream and finish
off flan).

7.15 Cook potatoes and make
sauce for fish.

7.45 Drain fish and keep warm
Reheat soup and thicken.

8.00 Serve first course.

Cream of beetroot soup

1 large beetroot (about $\frac{3}{4}$ lb)
— cooked, skinned and grated
1 medium-size onion (finely
chopped)
1 oz butter
$\frac{3}{4}$ oz plain flour
1$\frac{1}{4}$ pints well-flavoured chicken
stock
salt and pepper
1 teaspoon red wine vinegar
$\frac{1}{2}$ teaspoon mustard (ready-made)
1 dessertspoon cornflour
3 tablespoons cream, or soured
cream
1 tablespoon snipped chives
small croûtons of fried bread
(to serve)

Method
Cook the onion in the butter
until it is soft ; add the flour,
cook it a few minutes until it is
marbled in appearance, then tip
on the stock. Bring this to the
boil, add the grated beetroot,
season well and add the wine
vinegar ; simmer gently for about
20 minutes. Rub soup through a
sieve or purée in a blender,
and rinse out the pan.

Return soup to the rinsed-out
pan and season well with
mustard, salt and pepper as
necessary. Mix the cornflour
with the cream, add to the soup
and stir until it is boiling. Cook
soup for 3 minutes, then taste
for seasoning. Add the snipped
chives and serve with small
croûtons of fried bread.

Turbot with lobster sauce

3 lb piece of turbot

For court bouillon
2 pints water
1 teaspoon salt
9 peppercorns
1 onion (sliced)
1 carrot (sliced)
bouquet garni
1 tablespoon white wine vinegar,
   or juice of ½ lemon

For sauce
¾ pint béchamel sauce (made with
   1¼ oz butter, 1¼ oz plain flour,
   ¾ pint flavoured milk)
lobster butter (made with 2 oz
   butter and lobster coral, or spawn)
diced lobster meat from ½ lobster,
   or 1 can of lobster
1-2 tablespoons double cream

The turbot can be cooked and
served 'in the piece' or you can,
if preferred, order it from your
fishmonger cut in even-sized
steaks.

Method
Put all the ingredients for the
court bouillon in a pan and
simmer, covered, for 8-10 minutes. Then cool and strain.

Soak the turbot for half an
hour in cold salted water, then
drain it and place, white side
uppermost, in a pan or deep
dish ready for poaching. Pour
over the court bouillon and cook
on top of stove, just below
boiling point (allow about 10
minutes if cooking the fish in
slices and 45-50 minutes if
cooking it in the piece). Alter-
natively, poach in the oven at
350°F or Mark 4 (allowing 15
minutes for sliced fish).

Meanwhile prepare the bé-
chamel sauce ; when boiling,
draw it aside and beat in the
lobster butter piece by piece.
Then add the lobster meat and
finish with the cream. Reheat
but do not boil. Keep sauce hot
in a bain-marie until it is wanted.

Drain turbot well and dish up
on a napkin. Serve with plainly
boiled potatoes and the lobster
sauce separately.

Lobster butter
Pound the coral (or spawn)
of a cooked lobster with
an equal amount of butter.
Season and press through
a nylon sieve.

*Left : adding lobster to béchamel
sauce after beating in lobster butter.*

The finished turbot is arranged on a napkin and the lobster sauce is served separately

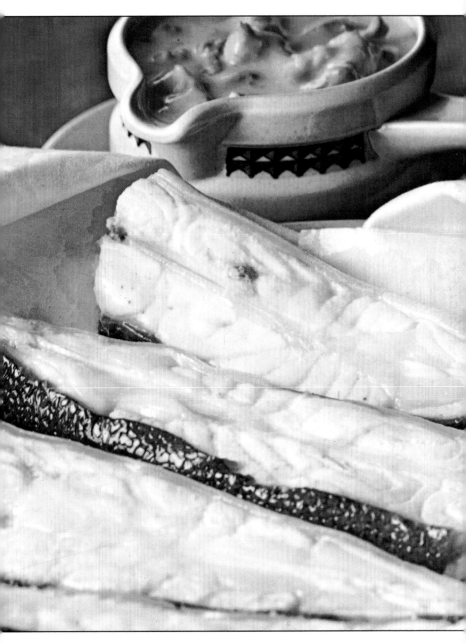

Pineapple upside-down cake

For topping
1 fresh pineapple
6 oz granulated sugar
¼ pint water
2 oz unsalted butter
6-8 glacé cherries
6-8 walnut halves

For cake mixture
4 oz butter
grated rind and juice of 1 orange
4 oz caster sugar
2 eggs (beaten)
5 oz self-raising flour
pinch of salt

*8-inch diameter moule à manqué,
or deep sandwich tin*

Method
Grease the sides of the tin only.

Peel and slice the pineapple and remove the core. Dissolve half the granulated sugar in the water in a frying pan over gentle heat. Put in the pineapple and cook very slowly until it looks almost clear. Do not allow the sugar syrup to boil hard or begin to change colour. Lift the pineapple from the pan with a fish slice and leave it to drain on a cake rack. Add remaining sugar to the frying pan with the unsalted butter and melt over gentle heat. Spoon this mixture into the sandwich tin and arrange the pineapple, slightly overlapping, over the butter / sugar coating. Decorate with the cherries and nuts.

Set oven at 350°F or Mark 4.

Soften the butter with grated orange rind, using a wooden spoon ; add the sugar and beat until light and fluffy. Then add the beaten eggs, a little at a time, and beat thoroughly. Sift the flour with the salt and fold it into the mixture with the strained orange juice. Spoon the mixture into the prepared tin and bake in the pre-set oven for 45-50 minutes. Test with a skewer, and when this comes out clean, invert cake immediately on to the serving plate. Leave for a few minutes, when the sugar mixture will run down over the cake. Then remove the tin.

Serve cake, while still warm, with a bowl of whipped cream or a hard sauce (see page 22.)

Spooning cake mixture over the pineapple, cherries and nuts

Dessert

Pineapple upside-down cake is served inverted, showing pineapple, cherries and nuts

Almond and raspberry flan Alternative dessert

$\frac{1}{2}$ lb fresh raspberries

For almond pastry
3 oz butter
1 oz shortening
6 oz plain flour
1$\frac{1}{2}$ oz ground almonds
1$\frac{1}{2}$ oz caster sugar
1 large egg yolk, or 2 small egg yolks
2-3 drops of vanilla essence
1-2 tablespoons cold water

For almond meringue
3 small egg whites
6 oz caster sugar
6 oz ground almonds

For decoration
$\frac{1}{2}$ pint double cream
caster sugar (to taste)
2-3 drops of vanilla essence
browned, shredded almonds

8-inch diameter flan ring

Method
First prepare almond pastry : rub the fats into the flour, add the ground almonds and sugar. Mix the egg yolk(s) with vanilla essence and water and add to the dry ingredients. Work up lightly to a firm paste and chill for 15 minutes.

Set the oven at 350°F or Mark 4. Line the flan ring with the pastry, prick the bottom lightly and cover with the raspberries.

To prepare meringue : whip the egg whites until frothy, add the sugar a little at a time and continue whisking until the mixture stands in peaks. Fold in the ground almonds. Spread the almond mixture over the raspberries and bake in the pre-set moderate oven for about 30 minutes.

When the flan is cold, cover it with the cream, lightly-sweetened, whipped and flavoured with vanilla essence ; decorate with the browned almonds.

Menu 17 Fish

Serves 4

Starter : Ginger and grapefruit cocktail

Main course : Fillets of sole Dorothea

Dessert : Apricot and almond strudel

Alternative main course : Escalopes de veau provençale,
Sauté potatoes

TIMETABLE

Day before
Make almond filling for
strudel.
Make tomato pulp and
béchamel sauce for the sole.
Make and bake strudel and
keep in an airtight tin.

Morning
Prepare grapefruit and chill
but do not fill.
(Prepare the aubergine
mixture and potatoes for
veal.)

Assemble the equipment
and ingredients for final
cooking from 6.45 for
dinner around 8 pm.

Order of work

6.45 Whip the cream to serve
with strudel.
Put ginger in grapefruit
and dish up.
(Cook potatoes for veal.)

7.15 Cook rice to serve with
sole, set aside in mould to
keep warm.
Put sole to poach.
Add the cream and tomato
to the béchamel sauce.
Keep warm in a bain-
marie.
(Cook escalopes and
warm aubergine mixture.
Dish up and keep warm.
Finish creamed or sauté
potatoes.)

7.45 Turn rice on to serving
dish, but do not remove
mould ; arrange fish
around.
Put strudel in oven to
warm, if wished.

8.00 Serve first course.

Remove mould and put
sauce on fish between
courses.

Ginger and grapefruit cocktail

Starter

2 large smooth-skinned grapefruit
about 3-4 stems of ginger in syrup
  (sliced or shredded)

Method

Halve and prepare the grapefruit (see page 80), removing
all the pith. Hollow the centre
slightly and then put 1 tablespoon of sliced ginger with a
teaspoon of the syrup in the
centre of each half. Chill and
serve in coupe glasses.

Serve ginger and grapefruit cocktail for a refreshing first course

Fillets of sole Dorothea

Main course

2 soles (1¼-1½ lb each) — filleted
squeeze of lemon juice
salt

For sauce
1 oz butter
1 oz plain flour
7½ fl oz milk (flavoured as for
  béchamel)
1 small carton (about 2½ fl oz)
  double cream
1 rounded teaspoon chopped
  truffle (optional)

For rice
5-6 oz long grain rice
1 small onion (finely chopped)
1 oz butter
good pinch of saffron (infused in
  2 tablespoons hot water)
½ pint fresh tomato pulp (well
  seasoned and flavoured)
about ¾-1 pint of good chicken,
  or veal, stock

Savarin, or ring, mould (2 pints capacity)

Coating poached fillets of sole with sauce after arranging them round the rice

Method
Butter the mould well, then prepare the rice. Soften the onion in the butter in a flameproof casserole, stir in the rice and cook gently for a few minutes. Then add the saffron, half the tomato pulp and three-quarters of the stock. Season, bring to the boil, cover and put into an oven pre-set at 350°F or Mark 4. After 10 minutes, look at the rice and add a little more of the stock if necessary. Return the casserole to the oven for a further 5 minutes when the rice should be dry and flaky.

Fill the prepared mould with the rice, press down lightly and keep warm.

Meanwhile skin the fillets, fold in two and lay them in a buttered ovenproof dish. Pour over enough water to cover them, add a squeeze of lemon and a little salt, cover and poach in the oven for about 10-15 minutes.

While the fish is cooking, prepare the sauce. Make a béchamel sauce with the butter, flour and milk in the usual way, and finish with the cream. Stir in enough of the remaining tomato pulp to give it a delicate tomato flavour and add the truffle.

Turn out the rice in the centre of a round silver or steel dish, surround with the fillets of sole slightly overlapping and coat with the sauce. Serve at once. (See photograph of finished dish overleaf.)

▶

Fillets of sole Dorothea continued

Fillets of sole Dorothea are served coated with sauce, surrounding a mould of tomato-flavoured rice. The fish may be garnished with truffle

Apricot and almond strudel   Dessert

¾ lb fresh ripe apricots
3 oz granulated, or caster, sugar

For almond filling
3 oz ground almonds
2 oz caster sugar
½ egg (lightly beaten)
2 good tablespoons double cream

For strudel paste
8 oz plain flour
pinch of salt
1 small egg
1 dessertspoon salad oil
4 fl oz warm water

melted butter
icing sugar (for dusting)

1 *Beating strudel until soft and elastic*
2 *Pulling the dough out on a tea towel until it is paper-thin*

Method
Split and stone the apricots. Slice each half into a bowl with 3 oz sugar. Combine the ground almonds, 2 oz caster sugar, egg and cream and mix to a smooth paste.

Make the strudel paste by sifting the flour with a pinch of salt into a warm bowl. Make a well in the centre and pour in the lightly beaten egg and the oil, mixed with about 4 fl oz of warm water. Beat well until the paste is thoroughly elastic. It should be really soft, but if it is too slack, add a little flour. When well beaten turn into a clean bowl, dust lightly with flour, cover with a plate and leave in a warm place for about 7-10 minutes. Set oven at 400°F or Mark 6.

Lay a large tea towel on the table and flour it lightly. Flatten the paste by rolling slightly, then lay it on the floured cloth. Leave for a further 5 minutes before starting to pull gently from the sides. When paper-thin dab the

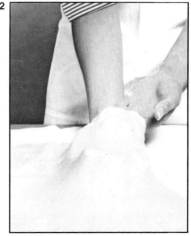

Apricot and almond strudel

top liberally with melted butter. Scatter over the apricots, then divide the almond filling over the top. Tilt the cloth to roll up the strudel, then tip it on to a wellgreased baking sheet, curling it slightly. Brush again with melted butter then bake in pre-set oven for 15-20 minutes, or until nicely brown and crisp. Take out and dust well with icing sugar.

Serve, preferably just warm, with a bow of lightly whipped cream

Escalopes de veau provençale

5 veal escalopes
2 tablespoons plain flour
  (seasoned)
2 aubergines (thinly sliced and
  scored)
4 large tomatoes
4 tablespoons olive oil (for frying)
1 clove of garlic (finely chopped)
1 teaspoon tomato purée
1 wineglass white wine
salt and pepper
8 black olives (stoned)
1 tablespoon chopped parsley

Method

Roll the escalopes in seasoned flour. Sprinkle aubergines slices with salt and leave for 30 minutes. Scald, skin and quarter the tomatoes and remove the seeds. Heat 2 tablespoons olive oil in a sauté pan and cook veal briskly for 3-4 minutes on each side, turning once, until golden-brown.

To make gravy, add the garlic to the pan, cook for about 1 minute, then add the tomato purée and wine. Season, cover pan and simmer for 7-8 minutes.

Meanwhile, wipe and dry the aubergine slices and fry in remaining 2 tablespoons olive oil for 2-3 minutes on each side. Add the tomatoes to the pan and simmer with aubergines until soft and pulpy, for 5-6 minutes, then add the olives.

Arrange the escalopes on a serving dish slightly overlapping. Boil up the gravy and spoon it over them. Arrange the aubergine mixture to one side or at each end of the dish, and sprinkle with chopped parsley. Serve with sauté potatoes.

Sauté potatoes

1½ lb potatoes
2 tablespoons oil
1 oz butter
salt and pepper
1 dessertspoon parsley
  (chopped)

Method

Scrub potatoes and boil in their skins until very tender. Then drain, peel and slice. Afterheating a frying pan put in oil, and when this is hot add the butter. Slip in all the potatoes at once, add seasoning and cook (sauté) until golden-brown and crisp, yet buttery, occasionally turning the contents of the pan. Draw aside, check seasoning, and add parsley. Serve in a very hot dish.

Appendix

Notes and basic recipes

Apricot glaze

This glaze can be made in fairly large quantities at a time, as it keeps well in a covered jar. It can be used with all yellow fruits.

To make 1 lb of glaze : turn 1 lb of apricot jam into a saucepan and add the juice from $\frac{1}{2}$ a lemon and 4 tablespoons water. Bring slowly to the boil, then simmer for 5 minutes. If glaze is to be kept, strain, return to pan and boil for a further 5 minutes before cooling and putting into a jam jar.

If you want to use it immediately, continue boiling until the mixture is thick, then brush generously over the fruit. If using a smooth jam (with no lumps of fruit) water is not needed.

Aspic jelly

This is a jelly made from good fish, chicken, or meat stock very slightly sharpened with wine and a few drops of wine vinegar. Care must be taken that the stock is well flavoured and seasoned and that it is not too sharp, only pleasantly acidulated.

With certain delicately flavoured foods, such as fish, eggs or prawns, home-made aspic adds to and enhances the flavour.

Aspic, and most jellies containing wine, will keep for several days in the refrigerator. To do this, pour the liquid aspic into a jug, leave to set, then pour about $\frac{1}{2}$ inch cold water over the top, and refrigerate. Remember to pour water off before melting the aspic for use.

Basic aspic recipe

$2\frac{1}{2}$ fl oz sherry
$2\frac{1}{2}$ fl oz white wine
2 oz gelatine
$1\frac{3}{4}$ pints cold stock
1 teaspoon wine vinegar
2 egg whites

Method

Add wines to gelatine and set aside. Pour cold stock into scalded pan, add vinegar. Whisk egg whites to a froth, add them to the pan, set over moderate heat and whisk backwards and downwards until the stock is hot. Then add gelatine, which by now will have absorbed the wine, and continue whisking steadily until boiling point has been reached.

Stop whisking and allow liquid to rise to the top of the pan ; turn off heat or draw pan aside and leave to settle for about 5 minutes, then bring it again to the boil, draw pan aside once more and leave liquid to settle. At this point the liquid should look clear ; if not, repeat the boiling-up process.

Filter the jelly through a cloth or jelly bag.

The aspic should be allowed to cool before use.

The stock for aspic jelly may be white (chicken or veal), brown (beef) or fish according to the dish being made.

Baking blind

A flan case should sometimes be pre-cooked before filling. Once the flan ring is lined with pastry, chill for about 30 minutes to ensure the dough is well set.

Now line the pastry with crumpled greaseproof paper, pressing it well into the dough at the bottom edge and sides.

Three-parts fill the flan with uncooked rice or beans (to hold the shape) and put into the oven to bake. An 8-inch diameter flan ring holding a 6-8 oz quantity of pastry should cook for about 26 minutes in an oven at 400°F or Mark 6.

After about 20 minutes of the cooking time take flan out of the oven and carefully remove the paper and rice, or beans. (Rice, or beans, may be used many times over for baking blind.) Replace the flan in the oven to complete cooking. The ring itself can either be taken off with the paper and rice, or removed after cooking. Once cooked, slide the flan on to a wire rack and then leave to cool.

Breadcrumbs

To make crumbs : take a large loaf (the best type to use is a sandwich loaf) at least two days old. Cut off the crust and keep to one side. Break up bread into crumbs either by rubbing through a wire sieve or a Mouli sieve, or by working in an electric blender.

To make dried crumbs : spread crumbs on a sheet of paper laid on a baking tin and cover with another sheet of paper to keep off any dust. Leave to dry in a warm temperature — the plate rack, or warming drawer, or the top of the oven, or even the airing cupboard, is ideal. The crumbs may take a day or two to dry thoroughly, and they must be crisp before storing in a jar. To make them uniformly fine, sift them through a wire bowl strainer.

To make browned crumbs : bake the crusts in a slow oven until golden-brown, then crush or grind through a mincer. Sift and store as for dried white crumbs. These browned ones are known as raspings and are used for any dish that is coated with a sauce and browned in the oven.

Butter, savoury

When these mixtures are made, either serve hot or pat into balls with butter 'hands' (wooden shaping boards), or spread $\frac{1}{4}-\frac{1}{2}$ inch thick on greaseproof paper and chill. Then cut into small round or square pats before using. The quantities given are enough for 4 people.

Anchovy butter

2 oz unsalted butter
4 anchovy fillets (soaked in milk to remove excess salt)
black pepper (ground from mill)
anchovy essence

Method

Soften the butter on a plate with a palette knife and then crush or pound the anchovies, adding these to the butter with ground pepper and enough essence to strengthen the flavour and give a delicate pink colour.

Garlic, butter

This is made in the same way, using 2 oz unsalted butter with crushed garlic, according to taste.

Château potatoes

1 lb old, or new, potatoes
1-2 oz butter
salt

Method

Old potatoes should be blanched before browning. Cut peeled potatoes into quarters lengthways, then use a potato peeler to trim off sharp edges (blanch, drain and dry). If using new potatoes, scrape and leave them whole, wash and dry them thoroughly, but do not blanch.

Melt butter in a casserole, add potatoes and cook over a moderate heat until golden-brown, shaking casserole occasionally to stop them from sticking. Season lightly, cover and put into oven to finish cooking for 10-12 minutes at 400°F or Mark 6.

Fondant icing

1 lb lump sugar
8 tablespoons water
pinch of cream of tartar

A sugar thermometer is essential for this recipe.

You can now buy blocks or packets of powder of fondant icing. Follow manufacturer's instructions.

Method

Place the sugar and water in a saucepan and dissolve, without stirring, over a low heat. Using a brush dipped in cold water, wipe round pan at level of the syrup to prevent a crust forming. Add the cream of tartar (dissolved in 1 teaspoon of water), place the lid on the pan, increase the heat and bring to the boil.

Remove the lid after 2 minutes, put a sugar thermometer in and boil the syrup steadily to 240°F. When it has reached this temperature take the pan off the heat at once, wait for the bubbles to subside then pour the mixture very slowly on to a damp marble or laminated plastic slab. Work with a wooden spatula until it becomes a firm and white fondant.

French dressing

Mix 1 tablespoon wine, or tarragon, vinegar with ½ teaspoon each of salt and freshly ground black pepper. Add 3 tablespoons of salad oil.

When dressing thickens, taste for correct seasoning ; if it is sharp yet oily, add more salt. Quantities should be in the ratio of 1 part vineger to 3 parts oil.

For **vinaigrette dressing** add freshly chopped herbs of choice.

Gelatine

As gelatine setting strength varies according to brand, it is essentiel to follow instructions given on the pack. For instance, Davis gelatine recommend 1 oz to set 2 pints of liquid.

Mayonnaise

2 egg yolks
salt and pepper
dry mustard
¾ cup of salad oil
2 tablespoons wine vinegar

This recipe will make ½ pint of mayonnaise.

Method

Work egg yolks and seasonings with a small whisk or wooden spoon in a bowl until thick ; then start adding the oil drop by drop. When 2 tablespoons of oil have been added this mixture will be very thick. Now carefully stir in 1 teaspoon vinegar.

The remaining oil can then be added a little more quickly, either 1 tablespoon at a time and beaten thoroughly between each addition until it is absorbed, or in a thin steady stream if you are using an electric beater.

When all the oil has been absorbed, add remaining vinegar to taste, and extra salt and pepper as necessary.

To thin and lighten mayonnaise add a little hot water. For a coating consistency, thin with a little cream or milk.

Eggs should not come straight from the refrigerator. If oil is cloudy or chilled, it can be slightly warmed which will lessen the chances of eggs curdling. Put oil bottle in a pan of hot water for a short time.

Watchpoint Great care must be taken to prevent mayonnaise curdling. Add oil drop by drop at first and then continue adding it very slowly.

If mayonnaise curdles, start with a fresh yolk in another bowl and work well with seasoning, then add the curdled mixture to it very slowly and carefully. When curdled mixture is completely incorporated, more oil can be added if the mixture is too thin.

Nuts

Almonds : buy them with their skins on. This way they retain their oil better. Blanching to remove the skins gives extra juiciness.

To blanch almonds : pour boiling water over the shelled nuts, cover the pan and leave until cool. Then the skins can be easily removed (test one with finger and thumb). Drain, rinse in cold water and press skins off with fingers. Rinse, dry thoroughly.

To chop almonds : first blanch, skin, chop and then brown them in the oven, if desired.

To shred almonds : first blanch, skin, split in two and cut each half lengthways in fine pieces. These can then be used as they are or browned quickly in the oven, with or without a sprinkling of caster sugar.

To flake almonds : first blanch, skin, and cut horizontally into flakes with a small sharp knife.

To grind almonds : first blanch, skin, chop and pound into a paste (use a pestle and mortar, or a grinder, or the butt end of a rolling pin). Home-prepared ground almonds taste much better than the ready-ground variety.

Pistachios : treat as for almonds but when blanching add a pinch of bicarbonate of soda to the water to preserve the colour.

Pastry

Puff pastry
8 oz plain flour
pinch of salt
8 oz butter
1 teaspoon lemon juice
scant $\frac{1}{4}$ pint water (ice cold)

Method
Sift flour and salt into a bowl. Rub in a piece of butter the size of a walnut. Add lemon juice to water,

make a well in centre of flour and pour in about two-thirds of the liquid. Mix with a palette, or round-bladed, knife. When the dough is beginning to form, add remaining water.

Turn out the dough on to a marble slab, a laminated-plastic work top, or a board, dusted with flour. Knead dough for 2-3 minutes, then roll out to a square about $\frac{1}{2}$-$\frac{3}{4}$ inch thick.

Beat butter, if necessary, to make it pliable and place in centre of dough. Fold this up over butter to enclose it completely (sides and ends over centre like a parcel). Wrap in a cloth or piece of grease-proof paper and put in the refrigerator for 10-15 minutes.

Flour slab or work top, put on dough, the join facing upwards, and bring rolling pin down on to dough 3-4 times to flatten it slightly.

Now roll out to a rectangle about $\frac{1}{2}$-$\frac{3}{4}$ inch thick. Fold into three, ends to middle, as accurately as possible, if necessary pulling the ends to keep them rectangular. Seal the edges with your hand or rolling pin and turn pastry half round to bring the edge towards you. Roll out again and fold in three (keep a note of the 'turns' given). Set pastry aside in refrigerator for 15 minutes.

Repeat this process, giving a total of 6 turns with a 15-minute rest after each two turns. Then leave in the refrigerator until wanted.

Watchpoint Always roll the dough away from you, keeping the pressure as even as possible.

Rough puff pastry
8 oz plain flour
pinch salt
6 oz firm butter, or margarine
$\frac{1}{4}$ pint ice-cold water (to mix)

149

Method

Sift the flour with salt into a mixing bowl. Take 1 oz of fat and rub it into the flour. Mix to a firm but pliable dough with the water, knead lightly until smooth, then set in a cool place for 10-15 minutes.

Place the remaining fat between two pieces of greaseproof paper and beat to a flat cake with the rolling pin. This fat should be the same consistency as the dough.

Roll out this dough to a rectangle, place the flattened fat in the middle, fold like a parcel and turn over.

Complete the following action three times : roll out dough to an oblong, fold in three and make a half-turn to bring the open edge towards you so that the pastry has three turns in all. Chill for 10 minutes, then roll out and use as required.

Praline powder

To make praline powder heat almonds and sugar gently in a small heavy pan. When sugar is a liquid caramel, stir carefully with a metal spoon to toast nuts on all sides. Turn on to an oiled tin and leave to set. When cold, crush praline with a rolling pin or put through a nut-mill, mincer or grater.

Redcurrant jelly

It is not possible to give a specific quantity of redcurrants as the recipe is governed by the amount of juice made, which is variable.

Method

Wash the fruit and, without removing from the stems, put in a 7 lb jam jar or stone crock. Cover and stand in deep pan of hot water. Simmer on top of the stove or in the oven at 350°F or Mark 4, mashing the fruit a little from time to time, until all the juice is extracted (about 1 hour).

Then turn fruit into a jelly-bag, or double linen strainer, and allow to drain undisturbed overnight over a basin.

Watchpoint To keep the jelly clear and sparkling, do not try to speed up the draining process by forcing juice through ; this will only make the jelly cloudy.

Now measure juice. Allowing 1 lb lump, or preserving sugar, to each pint of juice, mix juice and sugar together, dissolving over slow heat. When dissolved, bring to the boil, boil hard for 3-5 minutes and skim with a wooden spoon. Test a little on a saucer ; allow jelly to cool, tilt saucer and, if jelly is set, it will wrinkle. Put into jam jars, place small circles of greaseproof paper over jelly, label and cover with jam pot covers. Store in a dry larder until required.

Redcurrant glaze

Home-made redcurrant jelly is best as it gives the right sharpness of flavour to the fresh fruit. Beat the jelly with a fork or small whisk until it liquefies, then rub through a strainer into a small saucepan. Heat gently without stirring until quite clear (boiling will spoil both colour and flavour). When brushing this glaze over the fruit use a very soft brush. Always work from the centre outwards, drawing the brush well laden with the glaze towards the edge.

Rice (boiled)

There are almost as many ways of cooking rice as there are cooks, so if you have your own well-tried method stick to it, but if you have problems, the following method is foolproof.

Allow 2 oz of washed rice per person.

Shower the rice into a large pan of boiling, salted water, at least 3 quarts for 8 oz, and add a slice of lemon for flavour. Stir with a fork to prevent sticking and boil steadily for about 12 minutes until tender. Rice very quickly overcooks so watch its cooking time carefully.

To stop rice cooking, tip it quickly into a colander and drain, or pour $\frac{1}{2}$ cup of cold water into the pan and drain in a colander.

Then pour over a jug of hot water to wash away remaining starch, making several holes through the rice (with the handle of a wooden spoon) to help it drain more quickly. Turn on to a large meat dish and leave in a warm place dry.

Turn rice from time to time with a fork.

For easy reheating, spoon rice into a well buttered, shallow oven-proof dish which should be small enough for the rice to fill it amply. Place a sheet of well-buttered paper over the top. The rice can then be reheated and served in this dish. Allow 30 minutes in the oven at 350°F or Mark 4.

Sauces

Béchamel sauce
$\frac{1}{2}$ pint milk
1 slice of onion
1 small bayleaf
6 peppercorns
1 blade of mace

For roux
$\frac{3}{4}$ oz butter
1 rounded tablespoon plain flour
salt and pepper

Method
Pour milk into a saucepan, add the flavourings, cover pan and infuse on gentle heat for 5-7 minutes. Strain milk and set it aside. Rinse and wipe cut the pan and melt the butter in it. Remove pan from heat and stir in the flour to make a soft, semi-liquid roux.

Pour on half the milk and blend until smooth, using a wooden spoon. Add rest of milk and season lightly. Return pan to heat and stir until boiling. Boil for no longer than 2 minutes.

Demi-glace sauce
3 tablespoons salad oil
1 small onion (finely diced)
1 small carrot (finely diced)
$\frac{1}{2}$ stick of celery (finely diced)
1 rounded tablespoon plain flour
1 teaspoon tomato purée
1 tablespoon mushroom peelings (chopped), or 1 mushroom
1 pint well-flavoured brown stock (see page 152)
bouquet garni
salt and pepper

Method
Heat a saucepan, put in the oil and then add diced vegetables (of which there should be no more than 3 tablespoons in all). Lower heat and cook gently until vegetables are on point of changing colour ; an indication of this is when they shrink slightly.

Mix in the flour and brown it slowly, stirring occasionally with a metal spoon and scraping the flour well from the bottom of the pan. When it is a good colour draw pan aside, cool a little, add tomato purée and chopped peelings or mushroom, $\frac{3}{4}$ pint of cold stock bouquet garni and seasonings.

Bring to the boil, partially cover pan and cook gently for about 35-40 minutes. Skim off any scum which rises to the surface during this time. Add half the reserved stock, bring again to boil and skim. Simmer for 5 minutes. Add rest of stock, bring to boil and skim again.

Watchpoint Addition of cold stock accelerates rising of scum and so helps to clear the sauce.

Cook for a further 5 minutes, then strain, pressing vegetables gently to extract the juice. Rinse out the pan and return sauce to it. Partially cover and continue to cook gently until syrupy in consistency.

Mornay (cheese) sauce

Make ½ pint white or béchamel sauce, remove from heat and gradually stir in 2-3 rounded tablespoons grated cheese. When well mixed, add ½ teaspoon made mustard. Reheat but do not boil.

Steaming

To steam puddings, turn the mixture into a well greased pudding basin and cover with buttered greaseproof paper and foil. Make two 1-inch pleats in the centre of both greaseproof and foil, at right angles to each other, to allow the pudding to rise. Tie down with string.

Have ready a saucepan with sufficient boiling water to come half way up the basin. Put the basin in the water and steam for the length of time stated in the recipe. Keep the water boiling all the time and make sure that the saucepan doesn't boil dry.

Stocks
Brown bone stock

3 lb beef bones (or mixed beef veal)
2 onions (quartered)
2 carrots (quartered)
1 stick of celery (sliced)
large bouquet garni
6 peppercorns
3-4 quarts water
salt

6-quart capacity saucepan, or small fish kettle

Method

Wipe bones but do not wash unless unavoidable. Put into a very large pan. Set on gentle heat and leave bones to fry gently for 15-20 minutes. Enough fat will come out from the marrow so do not add any to pan unless bones are very dry. After 10 minutes add the vegetables.

When bones and vegetables are just coloured, add herbs, peppercorns and the water, which should come up two-thirds above level of ingredients. Bring slowly to the boil, skimming occasionally, then half cover pan and simmer 4-5 hours, or until stock tastes strong and good.

Strain off and use bones again for a second boiling. Although this second stock will not be so strong as the first, it is good for soups and gravies. Use the first stock for brown sauces, sautés, casseroles, or where a jellied stock is required. For a strong beef broth, add 1 lb shin of beef to the pot halfway through the cooking.

Chicken stock

This should ideally be made from the giblets (neck, gizzard, heart and feet, if available), but never the liver which imparts a bitter flavour. This is better kept for making pâté, or sautéd and used as a savoury. Dry fry the giblets with an onion, washed but not peeled, and cut in half. To dry fry, use a thick pan with a lid, with barely enough fat to cover the bottom. Allow the pan to get very hot before putting in the giblets and onion, cook on full heat until lightly coloured. Remove pan from heat before covering with 2 pints of cold water. Add a large pinch of salt, a few peppercorns and a bouquet garni (bayleaf, thyme, parsley) and simmer gently for 1-2 hours.

Note : for jellied chicken stock, use the raw carcass.

152

Fish stock
1 medium-size onion
$1\frac{1}{2}$ lb sole bones
$\frac{1}{2}$ oz butter
6 white peppercorns
small bouquet garni
juice of $\frac{1}{2}$ lemon
salt
2 pints water

Method
Slice the onion, blanch and refresh. Wash the sole bones well and drain them. Melt the butter in a large pan and put in the prepared onion, sole bones, peppercorns, bouquet garni, lemon juice and salt.

Cover the pan and put over very gentle heat for 10 minutes. Add the water, bring to the boil and skim well. Simmer gently for 20 minutes, then strain through a fine nylon strainer. Leave stock to cool ; when cold, cover and keep in refrigerator until wanted.

Veal (white bone) stock
3 lb veal bones
2 onions (quartered)
2 carrots (quartered)
1 stick of celery (sliced)
large bouquet garni
6 peppercorns
3-4 quarts water
salt

*6-quart capacity saucepan, or small
 fish kettle*

Method
Wipe bones but do not wash them unless unavoidable. Put them in a large pan with the water, bring slowly to the boil, skimming from time to time to remove fat. When the fat has been skimmed off the liquid, add the vegetables, bouquet garni and seasoning.

Simmer for 4-5 hours, or until the stock tastes strong and good.

Strain off and use the bones again for a second boiling. Although this second stock will not be as strong as the first, it is good for soups and gravies. Use the first stock where a jellied stock is required.

Vegetable stock
1 lb carrots
1 lb onions
$\frac{1}{2}$ head of celery
$\frac{1}{2}$ oz butter
3-4 peppercorns
1 teaspoon tomato purée
2 quarts water
salt

Method
Quarter the vegetables, and brown them lightly in the butter in a large pan. Add peppercorns, tomato purée, water and salt. Bring to the boil, cover pan and simmer for 2 hours or until the stock has a good flavour.

Sugar syrup (for stock)
Dissolve 1 lb lump, or granulated, sugar in $\frac{1}{2}$ pint water over gentle heat, then boil steadily, without stirring, until sugar thermometer reads $220°$ F. Allow syrup to cool, then store by pouring it into a large, clean and dry screwtop jar.

Tomato pulp
In season, use rather ripe tomatoes ; at other times of the year it is better to use canned Italian tomatoes. To make $\frac{1}{2}$ pint of pulp, take $\frac{3}{4}$ lb ripe tomatoes (seeds removed) or a 14 oz can. Put into a pan with a clove of lightly bruised garlic, a bayleaf, salt, pepper ground from the mill and a slice of onion. Add a nut of butter, cover and cook slowly to a thick pulp, about 10-15 minutes. When really thick, pass pulp through a strainer. Adjust the seasoning, adding a little sugar if it is too sharp.

Tomatoes (skinning and seeding)

Skin tomatoes, place them in a bowl, pour boiling water over them, count 12, then pour off the hot water and replace it with cold. The skin then comes off easily. Cut a slice from the top (not stalk end) of each tomato, reserve slices ; hold tomato in hollow of your palm, flick out seeds with the handle of a teaspoon, using the bowl of the spoon to detach the core. So much the better if the spoon is worn and therefore slightly sharp.

Vanilla sugar

Store a dry vanilla pod, or a few vanilla seeds, in a small jar of caster sugar. Keep well stoppered. This sugar may be used for flavouring cakes and custards.

Glossary

Bain-marie (au) To cook at temperature just below boiling point in a bain-marie (a saucepan standing in a larger pan of simmering water). Used in the preparation of sauces, creams and food liable to spoil if cooked over direct heat. May be carried out in oven or on top of stove. A double saucepan gives a similar result. Sauces and other delicate dishes may be kept hot in a bain-marie at less than simmering heat.

Baste To spoon hot fat / liquid over food as it cooks in the oven.

Blanch To remove strong tastes from vegetables by bringing to the boil from cold water and draining before further cooking. Green vegetables should be put into boiling water and cooked for up to 1 minute.

Bouquet garni Traditionally a bunch of parsley, thyme, bayleaf, for flavouring stews and sauces. Other herbs can be added. Remove before serving dish.

Butter, clarified Butter which is heated gently until foaming, skimmed well and the clear yellow liquid strained off, leaving the sediment (milk solids) behind.

Butter, kneaded Butter and flour worked together to form a paste (in the proportion of 1 oz butter to $\frac{1}{2}$ oz flour). It is used to thicken liquid and is added in small pieces, usually at the end of the cooking process. When the exact quantity of liquid is unknown this is the quickest way to thicken.

Croûte Small round of bread, lightly toasted or fried. It can be spread or piled up with a savoury mixture or used as a garnish.

Croûton Small square or dice of fried bread or potato to accompany purée or cream soups.

Deglaze To heat stock and / or wine together with flavoursome sediments left in roasting / frying pan so that gravy / sauce is formed. (Remove excess fat first.)

Glaze 1. To brown under the grill or in the oven. 2. To make shiny with egg, water or milk.

Infuse To steep in liquid (not always boiling) in a warm place to draw flavour into the liquid.

Julienne The cut size and shape of vegetables and garnishes for certain dishes. A julienne strip is usually about $\frac{1}{8}$ inch by $1\frac{1}{2}$-2 inches long.

Liaison Mixture for thickening / binding sauce / gravy / soup, eg. roux, egg yolks and cream, kneaded butter.

Marinate To soak raw meat / game / fish in cooked or raw spiced liquid (marinade) of wine, oil, herbs and vegetables for hours / days before cooking. This softens, tenderises and flavours, and a marinade can be used for final sauce. Use glass / glazed / enamel / stainless steel vessel to withstand effects of acid.

Reduce To boil a liquid fast to reduce quantity and concentrate the flavour.

Roux Fat and flour mixture which is the basis of all flour sauces. The fat is melted and the flour stirred in off the heat before liquid is added.

Salpicon The name given to a mixture of shredded ingredients usually bound with a rich sauce. This may be used as a garnish, a stuffing for pastry cases and other dishes, or be made into croquettes.

Sauté To brown food in butter, or oil and butter. Sometimes cooking is completed in a 'small' sauce - ie. one made on the food in the sauté pan.

Scald 1. To plunge into boiling water for easy peeling. 2. To heat a liquid, eg. milk, to just under boiling point.

Seasoned flour Flour to which salt and pepper have been added. To 1 tablespoon of flour add a pinch of pepper, and as much salt as you can hold between your thumb and two fingers.

Shortening Fat which when worked into flour gives a short, crisp quality to pastry / cakes. Fats with least liquid, e.g. lard, vegetable fat, contain most shortening power.

Index